The Complainer's Guide to Getting Even

The Complainer's Guide to Getting Even

Jasper Griegson

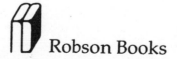

Robson Books

To Bettina, Nina and Zoë – three women
who really know how to complain

First published in Great Britain in 1994 by Robson Books Ltd,
Bolsover House, 5-6 Clipstone Street, London WlP 7EB

Copyright © 1994 Jasper Griegson
The right of Jasper Griegson to be identified as author of this work has
been asserted by him in accordance with the Copyright, Designs and
Patents Act 1988

British Library Cataloguing in Publication Data
A catalogue record for this title is available from the British Library

ISBN 0 86051 948 1

Designed by Harold King

Typeset by Harrington & Co., London
Printed in Great Britain by Butler & Tanner Ltd.,
London and Frome

Contents

Acknowledgements

Many thanks to News Group Newspapers Ltd for kindly allowing me to reproduce my *Sun* letters from the period when I was the Official Complainer for that newspaper.

Many thanks also to IPC Magazines Ltd for allowing me to reproduce my *Woman's Realm* letters.

Finally, thanks to all the companies who have responded generously and humorously to my letters of complaint.

Introduction

A few years ago I was given a box of liqueurs which a friend had purchased for me in Copenhagen. They were defective. Most people would have binned the chocs and forgotten about them. I didn't. I wrote to the manufacturers threatening to tie myself to the railings of the Danish Embassy and to flambé myself in liqueur unless I received justice.

However did I come to develop such a curiously aggressive attitude?

I am a complainer. I complain because life is too short. We live in an age when we are all constantly bugged by a myriad of irritants. Be it a holiday wrecked by a smelly hotel room, a glass of warm white wine at a restaurant or a mouldy digestive biscuit, life is a series of minuscule battles. Most people suffer in silence. I don't. I decided some time ago that there was only one way to deal with life's little problems and that was to enjoy them.

When I visited EuroDisney last Christmas I wasn't upset when I discovered that there was no hot water in our room. I was delighted. I knew that I had something to complain about and that moreover the cost of the holiday would eventually be refunded. It was.

I enjoy writing letters of complaint.

The primary source of my pleasure is the act of writing itself. It gives me an opportunity to indulge in creative writing, a diversion which most of us abandon when we leave school. My complaints are not just complaints as such. They are art. In the way that some people find solace in sculpture, painting or cutting their ears off, I find solace in venting my spleen on paper. There is surprisingly little of the Esther Rantzen in me. I'm not so much a consumer rights campaigner, more a demented poet with a penchant for getting even.

I also like complaining because it has produced some startling results. Cars, holidays and restaurant meals have all flowed from my belly-aching letters.

I hope that after reading this book you too will feel confident enough to start complaining just like me. Any complaints about this book should be addressed to Jeremy Robson, Robson Books Limited, Bolsover House, 5-6 Clipstone Street, London W1.

Sorry Jeremy.

1

Don't Get Mad Get Even

I started complaining in 1986. In the summer of that year my wife and I were waiting in a sweaty departure lounge at Dublin Airport for an Aer Lingus flight to Boston. The take-off had been delayed for two hours due to 'technical difficulties with the engine' when it was announced that the aeroplane would not be leaving for at least a further three hours. Some of our fellow countrymen slumped back in their bucket seats with resignation, took a deep breath and carried on-reading their magazines. Others became profoundly unhappy and vented their displeasure by whinging amongst themselves in a loud but impotent fashion.

We were sitting next to a huge American gentleman and his wife. Upon hearing of the further delay the man immediately transformed from an unremarkable passenger to a crossbreed between a werewolf and a prosecuting district attorney. He was not upset. He was mad with rage. Unlike us, he was not prepared to tolerate the indignity of passive acceptance. His eyes lit up as he instructed his wife to follow him. We decided to do the same.

He calmly, but firmly, started to impose himself upon people behind desks until he encountered someone of suitable seniority. He informed the official that he and his wife would be lunching at the best available restaurant and that the airport authorities would be paying for it. They were duly provided with a letter entitling them to a free slap-up meal. Following behind them, the hard work having been done, I meekly requested the same and was given it.

As I ploughed my way through my third helping of crêpe Suzettes a white shaft of light came down from heaven. I too was transformed. I too was no longer aggrieved. I had achieved my first taste of success and in the process had learned two important lessons:

- Complaining works.

- Free food tastes superb.

The Managing Director
Wander Limited
Kings Langley
Hertfordshire
WD4 8LJ   26th May 1992

Dear Sir

Options White Choc Drink

I wish to register a complaint of epoch-making significance.

Yesterday, sitting bored in my office, I sampled your above-
mentioned product. I was horrified to discover that in somewhat
stark contrast to all the other Options drinks this one was so
thick that it tasted more like Dickensian gruel than a pleasant
cocoa beverage. Adding insult to injury it piled 20 more
calories into my body than the normal sachet, thus making me
fatter than might otherwise be the case and consequentially,
unattractive to members of the opposite sex. I received a letter
this morning from my wife's divorce solicitors notifying me that
due to my humungous obesity (brought about in no small part by
your product) my wife no longer wants me.

In all the circumstances I look to you for (a) a detailed
explanation about the watery but calorific nature of 'Options
White Choc' and (b) a massive gesture of goodwill.

Yours sincerely

Jasper Griegson

WANDER LIMITED

WANDER

Station Road
King's Langley
Hertfordshire WD4 8LJ

Telephone: (0923) 266122
Telegrams: Ovaltinus King's Langley
Fax: (0923) 260038
Telex: 922747

Your reference   Our reference   28 May 1993   DEE/wgg

Dear Mr. Greigson

We thank you for your protesting prose of 26th May in regard to Options White Choc.

Dickensian gruel was far from our minds in the conception of this latest Options confection. Extensive research indicated the flavour more akin to liquid milky bar. Indeed, so enamoured were respondents of the velvety, mellifluous taste, that they deemed an extra 20 calories a small price to pay for such munificence. Since White Chocolate is derived from cocoa butter, the calorific penalty is, regrettably, unavoidable.

We are, of course, dismayed to learn of your impending divorce resulting from over-indulgence. Abstinence is a recommended course of action, in addition to copious quaffing of the enclosed. As a massive gesture of goodwill they may fall short of the mark; as a last ditch attempt to become a shadow of your current self we can attest to their efficacy.

Thanking you for your interest and hopeful of your continued consumption of our products.

Yours sincerely

Debra Eddy
Marketing Manager

Encl.

The President
The McDonald Corporation
McDonald Plaza
Oakbrook
Illinois 60521
USA   5th January 1993

Dear Sir

I wish to register a complaint of the most serious kind.

I am a life-long fan of McDonalds and in twenty years have never
had cause to complain. As far as I am concerned the Big Mac is
the embodiment of nutritional perfection, the Chicken McNugget is
worth its weight in gold and the McDonalds Thick Shake is second
to none.

That said, for the very first time, I did encounter a problem
last Sunday at your restaurant in Golders Green, London. Keen to
indoctrinate my 3½ year old daughter in the ways of McDonalds, I
ordered a McNuggets 'Happy Meal'. The sign behind the counter
advertised that a McNuggets Happy Meal would contain 6 nuggets.
When my daughter opened the Happy Meal box to discover that it
contained only 4 nuggets, she burst into tears. Naturally I
complained only to be told by the manager that the number 6 on
the sign had been marked through with a green pen!

*What is going on? Rationing? Is there a world McNuggets
shortage?*

In the circumstances, I would be most grateful for your kind
reassurance that my fears are unfounded.

I await, with Pavlovian expectation, your earliest response.

Yours faithfully

J. Griegson

Jasper Griegson

Telephone
081-883 6400

Facsimile
081-444 5377

Telex
295187

DX No: 52051 East Finchley

20th January 1993

Dear Mr Griegson

Thank you for your letter regarding your visit to our Golders Green restaurant, which has been passed to me as Market Manager, whose responsibilities include this restaurant.

Please accept our sincerest apologies for the confusion over the McNuggets. We have, after numerous research studies, decided to offer a four nugget Happy Meal instead of six. Our research revealed that six pieces were generally thought to be too much for young children, and that four nuggets, with a price reduction, was better value for money.

At the time of your visit our Golders Green restaurant had not yet received the new menu strip showing four nuggets. The manager should have pointed this change out to you, thus clarifying any doubts you had. I have now addressed this issue with the entire management team.

I apologise for the disappointment caused to your young daughter, and in order to restore her faith in McDonald's I have enclosed some toys and a voucher for a free Happy Meal.

Once again, please accept my sincere apologies for the misunderstanding, and rest assured, we are not rationing McNuggets, only responding to what our customers have told us.

Yours sincerely

MICHAEL GOMES
Market Manager

The Managing Director
J Lyons and Co Limited
Oldfield Lane North
Greenford
Middlesex   2nd August 1987

Dear Sir

Re: A Chocolate Cup Cake Surprise

I wish to register a complaint.

In the course of a recent visit to the Safeway Supermarket in
Pinner, I had the misfortune to purchase a packet of your
Chocolate Cup Cakes. The result of this acquisition can only be
described as an unmitigating hell. Upon opening the goods I had
no reason to suspect that a Cup Cake Calamity awaited me. I
ripped open the cardboard totally oblivious to the fact that
within the disarmingly attractive wrapping lurked a culinary
catastrophe.

To call the Cup Cake in question a Cup Cake at all amounts to a
grotesque distortion of the truth. The congenitally deformed
cocoa tart appeared to be no more than a gastronomic
reincarnation of the Elephant Man. In order to disguise its
hideously crippled shape, you its makers, endowed it with
THIRTEEN cups. This must surely be a record. Is it?

The amount of paper Cup I paid for was totally unacceptable. I
thought your company sold confectionery not stationery. I was
clearly deprived of an amount of Cake equivalent to the space
taken by the Cup. Please reimburse me accordingly.

I enclose the gateau's garments for your record.

Yours faithfully

Jasper Griegson

LYONS BAKERY LTD
Carlton, Barnsley, South Yorkshire S71 3HQ. Telex: 547479. Tel: (0226) 286191

7th August 1987

Enc: Reimbursement to the value of £1.50

Dear Mr Griegson

We were concerned to learn from our Managing Director that you had cause for complaint with our Chocolate Cup Cakes.

We are grateful that you have been willing to take the time and trouble to let us know of your dissatisfaction, and for giving us an opportunity to look into this matter.

We are very sorry that this product was not up to our usual high standard. The foil cases for our Cup Cakes are dispensed by machine. I have notified our engineering department so that a thorough check can be made into this problem.

Please accept our sincere apologies for the inconvience you have been caused. We would like you to accept the enclosed refund with our compliments and hope that this unfortunate incident will not deter you from buying our products in the future.

Yours sincerely

Mrs L Woodward
Consumer Relations

1 Virginia Street, London E1 9XP. Telephone: 071-782 4000. Telex: 262135.

8th April 1994

J Yaron Esq
El Al Airlines Limited
185 Regent Street
London
W1R 8EU

Dear Mr Yaron

I am the Sun Newspaper's Official Complainer and I write on
behalf of Miss R Knoble.

You are of course very familiar with Miss Knoble's recent crisis
involving breakfast in Tel-Aviv, lunch in London and luggage in
Odessa.

There would appear to be two possible explanations for the loss
of Miss Knoble's luggage for three weeks:-

1)   El Al luggage handlers' and security officers have been
     inept or

2)   Miss Knoble's luggage spontaneously developed a homing
     device and headed off to Odessa of its own accord in search
     of Miss Knoble's ancestors (who happen to have hailed from
     there).

I would be most grateful indeed if you would explain the
position. The sooner the Odessa file is closed and the
Compensation file opened the better.

Although (as her name suggests) Miss Knoble is blessed with many
virtues, patience is not one of them. She and I await your
earliest reply.

I thank you in advance for your interest.

Yours sincerely

Jasper Griegson

EL AL

REFERENCE	OFFICE	DATE
6001/100	VP & General Manager UK & Eire	13th April 1994

Dear Mr Griegson

Thank you for your letter of the 5th April and for its refreshing whimsical view.

The contents were certainly no secret to me, since I was personally involved in "masterminding" a successful rescue operation, together with Miriam Brandt (M?), the designated member of staff, and between us maintained daily contact with Miss Knoble.

I strongly favour the second of your possible explanations, in that, baggage handling and security at Ben Gurion Airport is not undertaken by EL AL staff. Miss Knoble's holdall could not be accepted as hand baggage, and had to be checked in. It was then that, either by virtue of a homing device or simply human error, it headed off for Odessa.

Airline baggage tracking systems today are very sophisticated and efficient, retrieving wayward cases with the minimum of delay. Thus it was quickly ascertained that the bag had not surfaced anywhere in the Western world. Despite 'glasnost' and 'perestroika', however, the former Eastern Block presented an 'Iron Curtain of Silence'. Only through the perserverence of a Russian speaking member of our Israel staff, were we able to trace the holdall in Odessa - alas several weeks later.

Miss Knoble was extremely relieved and most grateful, when she was notified that it was being returned to her with all the tapes, stereo recorder and microphone intact. She certainly gave no hint of seeking compensation. In any event, under the terms of the Warsaw Convention, there was no liability as no loss was suffered.

Consequently, as the matter was brought to a satisfactory and amicable conclusion, I am assuming that the Odessa file is now closed!

Yours sincerely

Jacob Yaron

I still treasure the silver bottle opener which Perrier gave me after my battle with them. I maintain to this day that Perrier bottles should bear a skull and crossbones to indicate the fact that Perrier contains trace elements of arsenic and cyanide. The mere fact that tap water has a similar composition is irrelevant.

The Managing Director
Perrier Water
UK Office
Aqualac (Spring Waters) Ltd
6 Lygon Place
London
SW1W 0JR

23rd April 1987

Dear Sir

Re Perrier Water That Tastes Like Water from the Paris Sewers

I enclose for your attention the top of a bottle which I purchased in 'Sandwich Plus', London EC4. To my amazement and horror the standard of Perrier water did not comply either with your normal very high standards or with the requirements of the Water Act 1972 Section 3(4)a.

Before I take the appropriate legal action I would be most grateful for a full explanation as to what happened, why and what steps you are presently taking to remedy the situation. The whole crate must have been bad.

Please send me a copy of the Officially Recognised Analysis of your product made on 23rd November 1984.

Love n' stuff

Jasper Griegson

Enc

Perrier (UK) Limited · 6 Lygon Place London SW1W OJR Tel: 01-730 0784 Fax: 01-824 8201 Telex: 917550
Registered office

27th April 1987

Dear Mr Griegson

Thank you for your letter dated 23 April, received by our office this morning, concerning an unsatisfactory bottle of Perrier.

Firstly, we would like to reassure you that this is a most unusual occurrence. Our factory in France is one of the most modern in Europe which operates under the strict regulations laid down by the French government. The highest standards of quality control are enforced, with each bottle subjected to a series of stringent tests throughout the production cycle. These include mechanical and electronic ckecks, as well as regular samplings taken at every stage of the bottling process to ensure that each bottle leaves the plant in perfect condition. We have total control over each stage of the bottle's production, which is why we are somewhat at a loss to explain how this bottle could possibly have escaped our quality control.

We would like to send a representative from Perrier to see you to discuss the matter further and to collect the bottle if it is still available. This will enable us to establish the possible cause of the problem. We would therefore be grateful if you could contact this office so that we may arrange a convenient appointment.

In the meantime, we hope this letter reassures you as to Perrier's highest standards of quality control and that you will continue to enjoy drinking our product.

We would like to thank you for bringing this matter to our attention and for allowing us the opportunity to make further investigations.

We hope you will accept the enclosed silver Perrier bottle opener with our best wishes. I also enclose a copy of the Perrier Chemical Analysis as requested.

I look forward to hearing from you.

Yours sincerely

Stephanie Pollard

STEPHANIE POLLARD
PR/CONSUMER AFFAIRS EXECUTIVE

encs: 1 silver Perrier bottle opener

BOUISSON BERTRAND INSTITUTE
Rue de la Croix Verte
ZOLAD
Route de Ganges
34100 Montpellier
France

Montpellier, 30 November 1984

Sample Received at Laboratory
on 24.09.1984 – Test no.84-9797

Springwater Naturally Carbonated
(Romans Source, Located at VERGEZE)
 Gard 30

FROM: The Technical Director
GSEMF
Usine of Vergeze
30 Vergeze

PERRIER

CHEMICAL TEST ON TREATED WATER

Resistance in ohms.cm at 20°C 1559

Conductivity in µs/cm^{-1} at 20°C 641

pH 6,0

Total Alkaline in ml N/10 57

Dry Residue at + 180°C .... 447,4 mg/l

Silica in SiO_2 .... 12,3 "

Bicarbonate in HCO_3^- .... 347,7 mg/l

Chloride in Cl^- .... 30,9 "

Sulphate in SO4 .... 51,4 "

Nitrite in N .... Nil "

Nitrate in N .... 3,6 "

Fluoride in F^- .... 0,08 "

Cyanide en CN^- .... < 0,005 "

Phosphate in PO4 .... 0,014 "

CO_2 disolved .... 6392,3 "

Continued ..../2

Calcium in Ca^{++} .... 140,2 mg/l

Magnesium in Mg^{++} .... 3,5 "

Potassium in K^{+} .... 1 "

Sodium in NA^{+} .... 14,0 "

Salts in $Li^{+\cdot}$ .... 0,005 "

Iron in FE^{++} .... < 0,020 "

Manganese in Mn^{++} .... 0,01 "

Copper in Cu^{++} .... < 0,020 "

Silver in Ag^{+} .... 0,005 "

Barium in Ba^{++} .... < 0,005 "

Ammonium in N .... < 0,05 mg/l

Cadmium ib Cd .... < 0,001 "

Chromium in Cr .... < 0,020 "

Lead in Pb .... < 0,001 "

Zinc in Zn .... < 0,020 "

Arsenic in As .... < 0,005 "

Selenium in Se .... < 0,005 "

CHEMISTRY, HEAD DIVISION

Ms S Pollard
Perrier (UK) Ltd
6 Lygon Place
London   8th May 1987
SW1W 0JR

Dear Ms Pollard

Thank you for your letter of 27th April.

As it happens, I have retained the bottle and its defective
contents. This matter is now in the hands of my solicitor from
whose offices the bottle can be collected. Should you wish to
collect the same please contact his secretary.

There were two points that concerned me regarding your reply:

1.   The analysis of Perrier shows against other things that it
     contains both arsenic and cyanide. Might this have accounted
     for the odd taste?

2.   You refer in the second paragraph of your letter to
     electronic 'ckecks'. How can I be sure that your elctrknik
     checks are satisfactory if you cannot even spell them
     correctly?

I thank you for your interst in my case.

Yours sincerely

Jasper Griegson

Perrier (UK) Limited · 6 Lygon Place London SW1W 0JR Tel: 01-730 0784 Fax: 01-824 8201 Telex: 917550
Registered office

SLP/MPM/8/OB4667

12th May 1987

Dear Mr Griegson

Thank you for your letter dated 8th May, received by our office this morning.

I have arranged with your secretary for our representative to collect the bottle of Perrier from Canon Street. Marie Obremski will be telephoning shortly to arrange a convenient appointment.

In answer to your queries regarding the analysis; you will note that the level of arsenic and cyanide present in Perrier is less than 0.005 mg per litre. EEC Regularions (EEC Journal L229 Vol.23 30 August 1980) state that the maximum is 0.5 mg per litre. The level of arsenic and cyanide within Perrier is therefore 100 times lower than the Maximum Allowable Concentration.

Obviously, until we have had the opportunity of analysing the contents of the bottle, it is impossible to determine the cause of the 'bad taste'. However, I am pleased to be able to reassure you that the traces of cyanide and arsenic would have no effect upon the product's taste.

Thank you once again for bringing this matter to our attention.

Yours sincerely

STEPHANIE POLLARD
PR/CONSUMER AFFAIRS EXECUTIVE

Your Ref: SLP/MPM/8/OB4667
Our Ref: Poisonous beverages

Ms S Pollard
Perrier (UK) Limited
6 Lygon Place
London
SW1W 0JR   20th May 1987

Dear Ms Pollard

Thank you for your letter of 12th May and for arranging for the
collection of my bottle and its contents. I trust you will let
me know the results of your tests. I am still concerned about
the hidden arsenic and cyanide that you sell to the unwitting
public. Despite your reassurances I feel strongly that the
arsenic and cyanide contents should be mentioned on a label on
the outside of every bottle.

Yours sincerely

Jasper Griegson

Perrier (UK) Limited · 6 Lygon Place London SW1W 0JR Tel: 01-730 0784 Fax: 01-824 8201 Telex: 917550

Registered office

SLP/8/OB4667

15 June 1987

Dear Mr Griegson

Further to the visit of our representative, Marie Obremski, to your offices, I am now able to inform you of the results of the chemical analysis carried out on the 330 ml bottle of Perrier.

The report states that 'The sample as received had a fairly heavy deposit of whitish material, both loose in the liquid and attached to the lower inside wall of the bottle. This crystalline deposit was shown to consist almost entirely of calcium carbonate.'

With the exception of the calcium figures, the chemical analyses is in good agreement with samples of Perrier water previously analysed by this laboratory. 'The calcium content of this water is about half that found in previous analyses, and this is due to the deposition of calcium carbonate crystals in the bottle. The most likely reason for this deposition is that the dissolved CO_2 gas has been allowed to escape from the bottle, but we cannot say where this occurred.'

It would appear that the calcium deposit is a result of the cap not fitting correctly, or being removed for an extended period of time. In either case, we would like to apologise for this unfortunate incident.

If you are agreeable, we would like to supply you with a complimentary case of Perrier. I would therefore be grateful if you could contact this office so that we may arrange a convenient delivery date.

Yours sincerely

Stephanie Pollard

Stephanie Pollard
PR/CONSUMER AFFAIRS EXECUTIVE

2

The Pen is Mightier Than the Sword

Notwithstanding my Heathrow Airport experience it is, on the whole, a waste of time complaining about a particular grievance on the spot. The only person who really gives a damn if Bloggs Biscuits taste crunchy is usually someone by the name of Bloggs who, in his or her role as managing director, is beyond the reach of ordinary mortals. The person least likely to be sympathetic to questions of crunchiness is Cynthia the shelf-stacker at Sainsbury's who, given the size of her pay packet, understandably feels less than wedded to notions of customer care.

No. The person to go for is Bloggs. Bloggs cares and the only way to make contact with Bloggs is by correspondence.

How do you get your letter through to the managing director? A lateral approach can produce results. A few years ago my life was plunged into turmoil by the arrival of my first daughter. Babies of the 1990s necessitate the acquisition of countless curious accessories such as sterilizers, perfumed nappy sacks and breast pumps. These items are invariably defective and fall apart or fail at the worst possible moment which, when screaming one month olds are involved, is most of the time. My wife bought a 'specially designed' bag from Mothercare, a product which claimed to make the task of carrying nappies and the like much easier. It didn't. It fell apart. Her hormones being in a state of serious unrest, my wife informed me that she wanted not only a refund but Sir Terence Conran's head on a silver salver, failing which she would make my life a misery. Knowing that the misery infliction process would include the hurling of metal objects at my nether regions, I set to work. To ensure that my missive reached its chosen target, I wrapped the offending nappy bag in the shape of a large missile and packed it off to Sir Terence. A substantial gesture of goodwill was immediately forthcoming. Albeit that I was unable to provide the chairman's scalp as a prize, my wife was thankfully placated and, as my second daughter will one day testify, my manhood was left intact. Another success.

The use of violence as opposed to the written word is generally a recipe for failure. This truth is illustrated by another salutary tale. A few years ago an Irishman called Tommy, who worked in my office, came to ask for some advice from the great complainer. He had bought a duff tape recorder from Dixons and wanted to know what to do. I was busy and impatiently told him that there was only one thing he could do. He should go immediately to Dixons' head office, ask to see the managing director and demand a refund. Tommy took my false pearls of wisdom at face value and duly proceeded to Dixons' HQ in search of justice. To this day I can still picture the scenario quite vividly in my mind. A man with a thick Irish accent carrying an electrical device wrapped in brown paper enters the building and asks to see the MD.... Needless to say, Tommy encountered some serious resistance in the form of three security guards. A scuffle ensued. Incredibly, they allowed him to leave his parcel and very shortly thereafter a replacement was provided. Tommy had discovered that personal confrontation is useless and unnecessary. The power of the poison pen is more than adequate.

Earlier this year a public debate was raging over the cancellation of a football match between England and Germany. The problem was that the game overlapped with the birthday of a short, dark Austrian whose hobbies included fishing, stamp collecting and world domination. Working on the assumption that the Führer had just had a bad press, I decided to intervene.

1 Virginia Street, London E1 9XP. Telephone: 071-782 4000. Telex: 262135.

20th January 1994

Sir Frederick Albert Millichip
Chairman
Football Association
16 Lancaster Gate
London W2 3LW

Sir Bert

I am the Sun Newspaper's Official Complainer and I write on behalf of a large number of our readers who have expressed their profound concern at the cancellation of the Germany v England match which had been scheduled to take place on 20th April.

The rationale for the decision is, I understand, that the fixture coincides with Adolf Hitler's birthday. I would be most grateful indeed for your explanation as to how this can possibly be justified and for your confirmation that the game will take place as planned.

On the assumption however that The Third Reich and international soccer are mutually incompatible I would draw you attention to a number of other birthdays which ought to be avoided: 12th January (Herman Goering); 19th March (Adolf Eichman); 17th June (Martin Bormann); 7th October (Heinrich Himmler) and 29th October (Joseph Goebbels). Venues to avoid include Nuremburg, the Black Forest and Dresden.

I look forward to receiving your earliest reply and thank you in advance for your concern.

Yours sincerely

J. Griep

Jasper Griegson

THE FOOTBALL ASSOCIATION
LIMITED
Founded 1863

Patron: HER MAJESTY THE QUEEN
President: H.R.H. THE DUKE OF KENT
Chairman: SIR BERT MILLICHIP

Chief Executive:
R. H. G. KELLY FCIS

Phone: 071-402 7151/071-262 4542
Telex: 261110
Facsimile: 071-402 0486

16 LANCASTER GATE, LONDON W2 3LW

Our Ref: FAM/SKB/197   *Your Ref:*   2nd February, 1994

Mr. Jasper Griegson,
The Sun,
1 Virginia Street,
LONDON.
E1 9XP.

Dear Mr. Griegson,

Germany v. England

I have your letter of 20th January, 1994.

The above match has in fact been postponed and discussions are now taking place with the German Football Association to find an alternative date and venue.

Yours sincerely,

Chairman

(Signed in the Chairman's absence)

1 Virginia Street, London E1 9XP. Telephone: 071-782 4000. Telex: 262135.

9th February 1994

H.R.H The Duke of Kent
York House
St James' Palace
London SW1A 1BQ

Your Highness

I am the Sun Newspaper's Official Complainer and I write to you
in your capacity as President of the Football Association. As
you can imagine, thousands of our readers are deeply disappointed
at the postponement of the Germany v England match due to take
place on 20th April.

I enclose for your attention an exchange of correspondence
between myself and Sir Bert Millichip, Chairman of the Football
Association. I'm sure you will agree with me that Sir Bert's
brief response fails to address the critical question raised by
me:-

     Why should the international footballing community need to
     arrange its affairs in such a way as to avoid key
     anniversaries in the Nazi calendar?

I would be most grateful indeed for the comfort of your support
for my view that this unmissable match should go ahead, as
originlly planned, on Hitler's birthday.

I await your earliest reply and thank you in advance for your
interest in this matter.

Yours sincerely

J. Criegn

Jasper Griegson

YORK HOUSE
ST. JAMES'S PALACE
LONDON S.W.1

14th February, 1994

Dear Mr Griegson,

The Duke of Kent has asked me to thank you for your
letter of 9th February but feels that this is not a matter
on which he can comment.

Yours Sincerely,

Nicolas Adamson

Private Secretary
Nicolas Adamson

Jasper Griegson, Esq.,

'Customer Services Departments' are not so much concerned with pleasing the customer as with apportioning blame away from themselves. Their last resort is to blame 'the Computer'. This pathetic excuse should be treated with the contempt it deserves.

1 Virginia Street, London E1 9XP. Telephone: 071-782 4000. Telex: 262135.

Lord Wolfson of Marylebone
Chairman
The Great Universal Stores Plc
Universal House
Devonshire Street
Manchester
M60 1XA   18th January 1994

My Lord

I am the Sun Newspaper's Official Complainer and I write on
behalf of one of our readers, Mr F J Allen.

Mr Allen and his wife are both in their eighties. They are
frightened and have asked for my help. The problem appears to be
a cybernetic monster ('the Monster') lurking somewhere within
your organisation (ref 045/06776572). The Monster would seem to
take one of two forms:

    1) It is either an overpriced uncontrollable computer
    which has nothing better to do than to threaten elderly
    people or

    2) It is an overpaid robotic employee with an undersized
    brain who has nothing better to do than to threaten elderly
    people.

In July 1992 Mr Allen bought some curtains from your company.
They were totally defective and so he returned them (see Arrow
Van parcel receipt no 6909554185). Despite this relatively
simple state of affairs the Monster continues to demand £133.01.
Mr Allen's attempts to communicate and reason with the Monster
have fallen on deaf Monster ears. Court proceedings have been
threatened.

Please arrange for the Monster to be summarily executed. I await
your earliest response.

Yours sincerely

Jasper Griegson

G.U.S. Home Shopping Limited, Universal House, Devonshire Street, Manchester M60 6EL Telephone: 061-277-4383 Telex: 668876 Fax 061-277-4904

Mr J Griegson
The Sun
1 Virginia Street
London E1 9XP

1 February 1994
Ref RR/JK/31.4

Dear Mr Griegson

re Mr F J Allen

Thank you for your letter addressed to Lord Wolfson in respect of
the problems that Mr Allen encountered with Great Universal.

It is apparent that whilst Mr Allen returned the goods via White
Arrow they have not been received in Great Universal's
distribution centre and I can only assume that they have gone
astray. We have telephoned Mr Allen and confirmed in writing
that his account has now been credited with the value of the
returned goods and that he will not be troubled further on these
matters. We have apologised to Mr Allen for the inconvenience
and I thank you for bringing the problem to our attention: as a
separate issue we are pursuing with White Arrow the location of
the missing goods.

I can assure you that there is no 'monster' lurking in Great
Universal and we do our very best to ensure that we deal with
cases like Mr Allen's as swiftly and efficiently as possible.

Yours sincerely

R REECE
Sales and Service Director

You may recall the battle which flared up a few years ago between the producers of champagne and a company which made a drink which it wanted to call 'Elderflower Champagne'. Naturally I had to put my oar in.

A W Gunn Esq
Pol Roger Limited
Landmark House
New Street
Ledbury
Herefordshire
HR8 2DX

18 August 1993

Dear Mr Gunn

I wish to register a complaint of the most serious kind.

Approximately three weeks ago I purchased a bottle containing an alcoholic beverage at the Tesco Superstore in Watford. The label on the bottle prominently featured the word Champagne, together with your name "Pol Roger". My dissatisfaction is twofold:-

(1)   I have always assumed that Champagne is a drink made from elderflower. Your product appeared to be completely devoid of elderflower. In this respect it must surely be said that the label was misleading if not disingenuous.

(2)   Having for many years been a consumer of Champagne (i.e. the elderflower drink referred to at (1) above) I have come to regard it as something of a refreshing tonic. Your product, in somewhat stark contrast, made me feel nothing short of bloody awful. Initially I became dizzy and thereafter I fell over which caused considerable pain and suffering to my temple. The morning after I developed a headache of spectacular proportions.

In all the above circumstances I look to you to restore my faith in your company and the quality of its products. Unless I hear from you with a positive response within seven working days I will assume that you accept that my above-mentioned complaint is both justiciable and meritorious.

Yours sincerely

J. Griegson

Jasper Griegson

Pol Roger Ltd.

19th August 1993

Dear Mr Griegson

Thank you for your letter of 18th August.

As you may imagine, we view such rare complaints as we receive with the utmost gravity, though yours is indeed an unusual one.

Perhaps I can respond by addressing the two sources of your dissatisfaction:

1.   Your assumption that Champagne is a drink made from elderflower is not, in fact, correct. It is, as any reference book will inform you, made from grapes. It may be of interest to you to learn, incidentally, that there is a body of opinion that Scotch Whisky is made from heather, and I have recently had occasion to correct this, not dissimilar, misapprehension.

2.   The symptoms you describe in your second paragraph are not such as would normally be associated with the consumption of our product. Perhaps the judicious application of your habitual beverage (the elderflower drink you refer to in your letter), cooled to a suitable temperature and applied by poultice to your temple, would have a suitably therapeutic effect, should the symptoms reoccur.

Trusting that these comments may be helpful, and assuring you of our best attention at all time, I am,

Yours sincerely

A.W. GUNN
Managing Director

3

Chronic Dissatisfaction

The paradox of being a complainer is that by never being satisfied you are always satisfied. Let me explain. When I buy a washing machine I know that I will end up being unhappy about its performance. My expectations are zero. When it goes wrong (as washing machines invariably do) I don't get distressed; instead I become almost serene. My writing hand starts to twitch a bit but not through anger. The inevitable has simply come to pass. My wife on the other hand is still able to foster the quaint notion that things work. When they don't she gets upset. She has expectations which are certain to be dashed. I don't and consequently I never get upset. Confusing but true.

My favourite come-on is the wording that tends to appear on the side of such consumables as chocolate bars: 'Please return this product if for any reason you are not entirely satisfied.' How can I possibly be 'entirely satisfied' by eating a bag of cheese and onion crisps? Perhaps if I were lying on a sun-drenched Caribbean beach sipping an ice-cold bourbon on the rocks having cheese and onion crisps fed to me by Sharon Stone I might be approaching 'entirely satisfied'. Otherwise not. The trick is never to be satisfied. Expect nothing and you will never be disappointed.

My personal raison d'être *is a passionate belief in life, liberty and the pursuit of chocolate. Given that my lust for chocolate is incurable I tend to get upset if the brown stuff is not exactly as it should be.*

Our ref: duff/chocs

9th April 1993

The Managing Director
Lessiters Limited
Hill End Farm
Hatfield
AL9 5PH

Dear Sir

I wish to register a complaint.

Earlier this week I became the proud owner of a chocolate pet rabbit (hereinafter referred to as 'Peter') purchased at your London city branch. In the course of what I can assure you was quite stable transportation, a calamity of myxomatosis proportions occurred: one of Peter's ears dropped off. I immediately attempted mouth-to-ear resuscitation but this was wholly unsuccessful. Having dismissed the notion of micro-surgery at Mount Vernon Hospital I decided to engage in a spot of do-it-yourself first aid. This also failed and, in fact, resulted in the loss of Peter's other ear. By this time he was starting to look more like a suicidal Dutch painter than an Easter bunny so I decided to calm myself down by eating his abdomen.

Despite having purchased your products for many eons this is the first time I have ever had cause to complain. In the circumstances I trust that you will wish to restore my faith in your company and the quality of its products. I enclose Peter's nose as proof of purchase. Let me assure you now that a dismissive two-line apology from your Customer Services Department will not suffice.

Yours faithfully

Jasper Griegson

Lessiter's LTD

Swiss Chocolatier

Hill End Farm
Mill Green
Hatfield
Herts AL9 5PH
Tel: 0707 268002
Fax: 0707 271769

29th April 1993

Your ref: duff/chocs

Dear Mr Griegson

Thank you for your letter of April 9th relating the most unfortunate accident that befell your newly acquired chocolate rabbit.

I would estimate from your description of the original injury that Peter sustained, that although the journey home was quite stable, he at some point suffered a sharp blow which caused his ear to fall off. The laws of gravity dictate that the ears are fixed to the head with a substantial amount of chocolate and only an impact of some force would cause them to be dislodged.

I was truly heartened by your heroic efforts to save Peter and I can only commiserate that your first-aid attempts were to no avail. However, in these circumstances neither mouth-to-ear resuscitation nor micro-surgery would be of any benefit, this unique type of rabbit needs specialist knowledge and treatment, usually involving the judicious use of heat.

Unfortunately these rabbits are renowned for their delicate nature and once they have suffered an injury of this magnitude the subsequent handling, particularly in unskilled hands, to try and save them can cause severe depression and they rapidly fall apart. The kindest course of action at this point is to dispatch them as quickly as possible, which of course you did.

I appreciate that Peter was very special to you and it will not be possible to replace him. However as token of our sympathy for this tragedy I have enclosed a box of our chocolates which I hope will give you some small measure of comfort and reassure you that all complaints are dealt with personally.

Yours sincerely

P Luder
Managing Director

Sir Graham Day
Cadbury Schweppes plc
1-4 Connaught Place
LONDON W2 2EX

24th June 1993

Dear Sir Graham

The Luxury Flake

I have seen the light. I am converted.

Tuesday, 22nd June 1993 will rank as the lowest day of my life. Why? Because on this day I sampled the most wonderful bar of Cadbury's chocolate ever but I did so in the knowledge that I may never sample such nectar again. I enclose the wrapper for your urgent attention. You will of course be aware that it is not made in this country but rather in New Zealand where chocolate seems to be decidedly creamier and far more delightful than anything produced here.

My plan is as follows: I would like to import boxes and boxes of luxury flakes en masse and set up a shop-cum-golden temple from which I could spread the word. A useful by-product of the exercise would be to make me and you very rich, very quickly. This money would also enable me (once I have eaten my way through the profits), to undergo counselling on chocolate addiction and also a serious programme of weight loss.

Please let me know what arrangements you can make to assist. I await your earliest response.

Yours sincerely

Jasper Griegson

Cadbury Schweppes

CADBURY SCHWEPPES
PUBLIC LIMITED COMPANY

From JOHN M. SUNDERLAND
MANAGING DIRECTOR, GROUP CONFECTIONERY

25 BERKELEY SQUARE
LONDON W1X 6HT
TEL: 071-409 1313
FAX: 071-830 5213
TELEX: 334413 CSPLC G

13 July 1993

Mr Jasper Griegson
36 Ashurst Close
Northwood
Middlesex HA6 1EL

Dear Mr Griegson

Thank you for your letter commenting on **Cadbury Luxury Flake** from New Zealand.

Our brands occasionally have different names in different parts of the world and you may not realise that we have a virtually identical product already on sale here in the UK.

This is **Twirl** which is also Cadbury Flake covered in Cadbury Dairy Milk Chocolate.

For this reason there is clearly not an opportunity for Luxury Flake in this country. However, we do appreciate the interest you have taken in our products and thank you for proposing such a novel idea.

I thought you might also appreciate a sample of our UK product **Twirl** with our compliments.

Yours sincerely

Victy than

JOHN M SUNDERLAND

Sir Adrian Cadbury
Cadbury Schweppes plc
1-4 Connaught Place
London
W2 2EX

8th January 1988

Dear Sir

I wish to record my profound disgust at the state of the box of
chocolates which I recently acquired at Heathrow Airport.

Having parted company with a wad of banknotes I rather expected
to encounter the high standards to which I am accustomed. I was
to be disappointed however because far from selling me 550g of
nutty chocolates you foisted upon me a rather tasteless
collection of cracked brown cannonballs. I enclose some examples
for laboratory analysis.

So outraged was I that I plotted the attached graph. The solid
line indicates the level of chocolate satisfaction which I
believe could and should have been reached. The dotted line
shows the harsh reality of the duff chocs.

Please compensate me by arranging for one of your juggernaut
lorries to stop off at my flat on its next outing from the
factory.

Yours faithfully

Jasper Griegson

CHOCOLATE
HAPPINESS

CHOCOLATE CONSUMPTION

Cadbury International Limited

the first name in chocolate

PO BOX 12
BOURNVILLE BIRMINGHAM B30 2LU
ENGLAND
TELEPHONE 021-458 2000
TELEX 338011 CADSCH G
FACSIMILE 021-458 2000 EXTN. 2244

L811/NSH/AL

19th January 1988

Dear Mr Griegson

Thank you for your letter dated January 8th which Sir Adrian Cadbury has passed to me for my attention.

I am sorry to learn about the poor condition of a 550g tin of Cadbury Nuts purchased at Heathrow Airport and can well understand your disappointment. This is a most unusual occurrence and I can assure you that an investigation will be underway at once.

Please accept my apologies for the inconvenience you have been caused and I hope you will accept a replacement tin of 550g Assorted Nuts with my compliments. I am arranging for these to be sent to you under separate cover.

Thank you for taking the trouble to write and advise us of this problem and I hope that your confidence in Cadbury will soon be restored.

Yours sincerely

N S Hawkins
MANAGING DIRECTOR

21st September 1993

Sir Richard Greenbury
Chairman
Marks & Spencer plc
Michael House
Baker Street
London
W1A 1DN

Dear Sir Richard

I wish to register a complaint of the most serious kind.

Although hanging was abolished in 1964, you appear to be making
efforts to re-introduce it. I enclose for your urgent attention
a neck tie which I purchased from your store in Watford. You
will see that the twist which appears to have developed in the
middle of the tie is somewhat reminiscent of the creaking rope
which used to be employed at the gallows. Unless I hear from you
to the contrary, you are likely to find me swinging from
Blackfriars Bridge as a protest against the merchantable quality
of Marks & Spencer's goods. You may wish to avert this
unpleasant public spectacle by either replacing the tie or
providing me with an appropriate refund.

I await your earliest reponse.

Yours sincerely

J. Griegn

Jasper Griegson

MARKS & SPENCER

REGISTERED OFFICE: MICHAEL HOUSE · BAKER STREET · LONDON W1A 1DN
FACSIMILE: 071-487 2679 · CABLES: MARSPENZA LONDON · TELEX: 267141
TELEPHONE: 071-935 4422

29th September 1993

Our Ref   ZER/980180/001/TC

Dear Mr Griegson

Thank you for your letter addressed to the Chairman. As a member
of the Corporate Affairs Group, I have been asked to investigate
the matter on his behalf.

I am sorry to learn of your recent disappointment with the tie.
We constantly strive to maintain and improve the standards of
quality which our customers have come to expect. It is therefore
disappointing to us when we hear that our merchandise is not
giving satisfaction.

I have discussed your comments with my colleagues in the buying
department concerned so that this matter can be referred to the
manufacturer.

Unfortunately, I am unable to send replacements from this office
and as I do not want you to be out of pocket (or suicidal!) I
enclose a refund for £10.00 to reimburse you.

Thank you once again for bringing this matter to our attention.
I hope that you will not be deterred from shopping in our stores
and that your future purchases will be entirely satisfactory.

Yours sincerely

Miss Zoe Raven
Corporate Affairs

4

If You Can't Beat Them, Confuse Them

If there is scope for coming at your target from an unusual angle, this is worth exploring.

If you are a scientist, blind them with science.

If you are a historian, blind them with some obscure chunk of history.

This tactic has worked for me on a number of occasions. Be it a completely irrelevant discourse on the Earth's orbit in relation to a malfunctioning refrigerator or a mind-numbing lecture on prehistoric man in relation to a problem at a car park, the principle remains the same. Dare to be different and by doing so distinguish your letter from those of the dull masses.

When adopting this approach, the following points should be borne in mind:

- Many people in authority suffer from what is called a fun by-pass. They do not respond well to wit and originality and should therefore be by-passed themselves. The worst offenders are middle-management types who work in the Customer Services

Departments of large companies. Customer Services Departments are what ordinary people would call Complaints Departments. Their mere existence is proof that the goods or services offered by the organization in question are frequently defective. The people who work in them are also defective. Avoid them.

• Your masterpiece of literature can be embellished by an unusual format. I once bought a music cassette from WH Smith which decided to chew itself up the first time I played it. I wrote a very straightforward letter to the managing director but did so in the style of a blackmail note using letters cut out from a magazine. This elicited a swift and positive reply. On other occasions I have written in a medieval style or in verse in order to attract attention. I have often thought about writing in blood but I am waiting for the right complaint to come along. I suspect that when it does, the red stuff will work wonders.

• The Hitchcock approach of keeping the reader in suspense until the final paragraph is another useful ploy. I once went through a sock bought from Marks & Spencer after wearing it for a mere 45 minutes. Naturally I did not wish to avail myself of the Customer Services desk at my local store. That would have involved queuing with everyone else, a concept which makes me shudder just to contemplate. Instead, I sent a letter to the chairman describing in great anatomical detail the peculiarly normal state of my feet. This produced an excellent result either (a) because the suspense was so great that the final revelation (my complaint) carried such impact or (b) because I had bored the poor man into submission.

The Customer Relations Manager
Marks and Spencer plc
Michael House
Baker Street
London W1   8th August 1987

Dear Sir

I am not the sort of person who normally complains but I must say
I feel honour-bound on this occasion to express my deep
disapprobation in writing. I have purchased goods at your stores
for very many years and have never had cause to be dissatisfied
in any way at all. I am fully aware that in the ordinary course
of events your wares are thoroughly checked by your no doubt
expertly-trained quality control personnel. This time however
somebody has failed to apply your usual strict standards since
the product which I purchased was of anything but merchantable
quality.

I would like to inform you by way of background material that the
following explanations cannot be put forward in your defence or
by way of mitigation: (a) I do not possess sharpened toenails;
(b) I do not suffer from any pedestrial deformities; (c) I am not
cloven-hooved or web-footed; (d) my tootsies are in perfect
working order; (e) there is nothing wrong with my trotters; (f)
my pedal extremities are pucker; (g) I do not possess talons; (h)
the nether digits in my lower limbs are quite normal; (i) my
beetle-crushers are exquisitely average; (j) the substructure of
my paws is beyond reproach; (k) I am not club-footed or club-toed
and I do not belong to any clubs that could in any way diminish
the magnitude of my claims against you; (l) I do not possess
claws; (m) I am pediferous in the most normal sense of the word.

In summary of the above I would conclude that my toes and feet
were beyond incrimination as regards the defect in question. I
enclose for your immediate attention a brand new sock with a hole
in it, together with my receipt. This should not have occurred
after one day's wear but it did. I see no reason why I should
have to suffer the inconvenience of having to return to Marble
Arch.

I look to you for a laboratory analysis and a gesture of
goodwill.

Yours faithfully

J. Griegson

Jasper Griegson

Marks and Spencer p.l.c.

REGISTERED NO. 214436
(ENGLAND AND WALES)

Date as postmark
Our Ref:
CR/MB/BI/18/08/MG

Dear Mr Griegson

Thank you for returning your sock
which I am sorry you have found
disappointing.

After examination, I have been unable
to determine the cause of the fault.
As I am unable to send replacements
from this office, I have pleasure in
enclosing a refund for £3.00 in gift
vouchers inclusive of postage.

I hope you will continue to buy St.
Michael products and that you will
find them to be of the high quality we
try to maintain.

Yours sincerely

C Richardson

MRS C RICHARDSON
Customer Services

The Customer Relations Manager
Birds Eye Walls Limited
Walton-on-Thames
Surrey

28th July 1987

Dear Sir

I write to express my deep dismay at the quality of your 'Black Forest Cake' a sample of which I purchased at the Tesco Superstore in Neasden last week. (Copy box enclosed for your attention). The box was perfectly intact and showed no signs of having been subjected to undue external disturbance but in somewhat stark contrast the contents resembled the creature from that 1950's science fiction film 'The Blob'.

The Blob was principally white with an infection of chocolate brownness spattered across it. Five members of my family tried to squeeze the Blob into a box to send you but its white tentacles clawed their way out whenever we pressed too hard on one side.

The extra-terrestrial gateau is available for inspection should you wish to make an appointment.

Please let me know if the cake is supposed to look like a suntanned heap of solidified shaving foam. If not, I would like to exercise my statutory rights as an aggrieved consumer since so far I have received nothing more for my money than aggravation and a half-melted alien.

Faithfully yours

Jasper Griegson

BIRDS EYE WALL'S LIMITED
Station Avenue, Walton-on-Thames, Surrey KT12 1NT
Telephone: Walton-on-Thames 228888
Telex: 261255

EI/MMMQ/BFC

4 August 1987

Dear Mr Griegson

Thank you very much for letting us know of your unsatisfactory purchase. May I offer my sincere apologies on behalf of the Company for any inconvenience caused.

The most stringent controls are enforced by the Company to ensure our products are of a very high standard. Frozen food, if kept at the correct low temperature, will keep for an indefinite period. In this case, it would appear that at some stage after leaving the Producing Factory, the product has been subjected to temperature abuse.

I would like to reassure you of the high quality of our foods by asking you to use the enclosed Voucher to purchase a further product.

Yours sincerely

M M McQueen (Mrs)
Consumer Service Supervisor

There is no reason to limit your complaints to defective confectionery and broken videos. Why not have a go at some of the bigger issues? Taking the stance that justice must not only be seen to be done but must be seen to be believed, I committed my views to paper.

1 Virginia Street, London E1 9XP. Telephone: 071-782 4000. Telex: 262135.

The Rt. Hon. the Lord Mackay of Clashfern
The Lord High Chancellor
House of Lords
London   8th December 1993
SW1A 0PW

Dear Lord Mackay

I am the Sun Newspaper's official complainer and I write on behalf of a number of our readers who have become concerned about a small matter on which you may be able to assist.

Standing outside the Old Bailey and looking upwards it would appear that the scales of justice have started to tilt slightly out of kilter. The imbalance is particularly noticeable from High Holborn and St Pauls.

I don't know if you have also noticed this phenomenon but I would be grateful if you could look into the matter and let me have your views.

My theory is that the tilting has occurred as a result of the recent decision in the Roger Levitt trial, the significance of which would appear to be that justice must not only be seen to be done, it must be seen to be believed. Woe betide anyone who steals a 34p tin of beans from Sainbury's but spirit away £34 million and you're laughing. Do you agree? I would be particularly grateful for any words of advice which you may wish to give to Britain's budding fraudsters.

I thank you in advance for your assistance.

Yours sincerely

J. Griegson

Jasper Griegson

HOUSE OF LORDS,
LONDON SW1A 0PW

Ref: C.41

21 January 1994

Dear Mr Gruegson,

    The Lord Chancellor has asked me to thank you for your letter of 8 December, in which you refer to the case of Roger Levitt, and to reply on his behalf. I am sorry that you have had to wait so long for a response.

    In your letter you draw a comparison between the sentence passed on Roger Levitt and a hypothetical case of theft. Such comparisons are frequently misleading since the full background to the different cases may be unknown. A considered, objective assessment of the circumstances of each individual case is made by the judge who is in possession of all facts of the case and after he or she has heard all that has been argued on behalf of a defendant in mitigation.

    So far as the scales on the Central Criminal Court are concerned it may be that the position from which you viewed them resulted in a distorted perspective. I can assure you that they are evenly balanced.

Yours sincerely,

M E Ormerod

1 Virginia Street, London E1 9XP. Telephone: 071-782 4000. Telex: 262135.

T. Murphy Esq.
Managing Director
Civil Aviation Authority
CAA House
45-59 Kingsway
London WC2B 6TB

7th February 1994

Dear Mr Murphy

I am the Sun Newspaper's Official Complainer and I write on behalf of the inhabitants of Festing Road, Putney.

The problem in essence is this. On an average day a large number of very big aeroplanes fly low directly over Festing Road making a loud din. The aircraft in question appear to be landing at what one can only assume is Heathrow Airport.

The good residents of Festing Road have has enough of raucous jumbos and have asked me to give vent to their deep seated unhappiness.

In all the circumstances I would be grateful if you could arrange for the relevant flight path to be changed and for Festing Road to be given a bit of a break. If the flight path could be shifted a few hundred yards to the left (say to Felsham Road or Redgrave Road) that would do nicely.

I trust this will not cause too much inconvenience and I thank you in advance for your assistance.

Yours sincerely

Jasper Griegson

Civil Aviation Authority
CAA House
45–59 Kingsway
London WC2B 6TE

Telephone: 071-379 7311
Direct Dial: 071-832 5767
Facsimile: 071-379 3264

Tom Murphy CBE
Managing Director

15 February 1994

Mr Jasper Griegson
The Sun
1 Virginia Street
LONDON   E1 9XP

Dear Mr Griegson

You wrote to me on 7 February 1994 about disturbance from aircraft flying over Festing Road, Putney. I am sure you would not want me to hold out false hopes to the residents, so I will try to explain the current situation and why there is no scope for altering it.

Festing Road is very close to the centre line of the Instrument Landing System (ILS) for Heathrow Airport's Runway 27 Left. The ILS is a landing aid providing pilots with guidance to the runway and it uses a beam known as the "localiser", which radiates from the far end of the runway along the centre. Obviously its position is determined by that of the runway.

In addition, another ILS beam known as the "glide path", gives the angle of approach to the runway, which for Runway 27 Left, is 3 degrees. As a result, aircraft over Festing Road are at approximately 2,400 feet, having to be established on the ILS at least 7 miles from touch-down.

Although very close to the centre of Runway 27 Left ILS, Festing Road is also a little less than one mile south of the centre line of Runway 27 Right. When the winds are from the west, which is most of the time, the two runways are used alternately with the changeover happening during the afternoon. This is done to bring some relief to local people.

I am sorry the residents of Festing Road are disturbed by aircraft noise but as I hope I have explained, there is very little that can be done to improve matters.

Yours sincerely

R H Armitage Esq
Bryant and May Limited
PO Box 57
Totteridge Road
High Wycombe
Bucks
HP13 6EJ   10th November 1987

Dear Sir

I am sure that you are a terribly busy and overworked man but I
would be most grateful if you would permit me to interrupt your
train of thought for a scintilla temporis. As a great lover of
your traditional Swan Vesta matches I write to add my name to the
swelling ranks of those who object to the recent change you have
made to the side of the packet. As you well know you have
committed an act of appalling artistic vandalism by replacing the
old swan with a different one.

The old swan had a style and elegance that one could associate
with the neo-Vermeer Dutch School of fine realism. It
encapsulated a whole world of Great Masters and afforded a great
dignity and serenity to the side of your cardboard boxes. The
new swan, in somewhat venomous contrast, is cheap, over-colourful
and basically revamps the old picture in what I would term
'Woolworths Impressionism'. Why you have decided to condemn what
had been a beautiful picture to the rubbish heap of history
escapes me. I attach a petition of all paid up members of the
BBSS (Bring Back the Swan Society).

I look forward to receiving notification from you that you have
reversed your earlier decision.

Yours faithfully

Jasper Griegson

By appointment to H M The Queen
Bryant & May Ltd High Wycombe
Match Manufacturers

Bryant & May Limited

Sword House   Totteridge Road
High Wycombe   Bucks HP13 6EJ
High Wycombe (STD 0494) 33300
Telex 837234

12 November 1987

Dear Mr Griegson

Thank you very much for your comments on SWAN. Very
disappointing to hear from a committed SWAN user as we spent a
great deal of time in testing how we could update the box to
better fit today's market.

We did consider many ways of doing this and finally selected a
short list of designs which we tested with a consumer panel of
SWAN users.

I have to say that there was unanimous enthusiasm for the
selected design which confirmed our decision to go ahead.

I am sorry that I cannot agree with your views but I hope you
will not be so put off to stop being a SWAN user.

Perhaps the enclosed cover will help!

Thank you for your comments. We are always pleased to hear from
anyone who has any comment whatsoever to make about our product.

Yours sincerely

R H Armitage
Chairman and Managing Director

For many years now I have been striving to write the Perfect Letter of Complaint. This letter is as close as I've got so far.

Managing Director
Harrods
Knightsbridge
London SW3

13th August 1987

Dear Sir

For many years now I have been a regular customer at your store
and have had absolutely no reason to complain. This however
really is the last straw and it is with deep dismay that I feel
honour-bound to write to you in this manner. After the events
which took place on the occasion of my last visit it rather seems
as though things are getting completely out of hand and I would
like to know what steps, if any, are currently being taken to
rectify the position. I had always thought in the past that your
store truly offers the kind of things it should but recent
occurrences suggest that this can no longer really be considered
the case. This is so particularly in the light of what is
happening at the moment. One is tempted to question how long
these developments have been going on, how long they can possibly
continue but more to the point, how they can be stopped. It is
undoubtedly the responsibility of all those concerned, both in
management and indeed on the shop-floor, to monitor the whole
situation very carefully. It may be a question of staff
training. From a personal standpoint I feel the substantive
situation must be checked. It has gone on for too long. As I
understand the position your store has always prided itself in
the utility it offers to the public at large, many of whom come
from far afield and who regard your store as a symbol of all it
should be.

I remain to be convinced that Harrods is what it once was and is
what we all think it is supposed to be. I look to you to restore
my faith in remaining the loyal customer I am, in the future.

Yours faithfully

Jasper Griegson

HARRODS LIMITED

KNIGHTSBRIDGE LONDON SW1X 7XL

TELEPHONE 01-730 1234 TELEX 24319 FAX 01-581 0470 REGISTERED OFFICE 87/135 BROMPTON ROAD, LONDON SW1X 7XL REGISTERED IN LONDON NO 30209

25th August 1987

Dear Mr Griegson

Thank you for your letter of 13th August.

I would apologise for the disruption caused by our refurbishment. We realise only too well that this is detrimental to our trading practice, but we do feel that the end will more than justify the means. It is anticipated that the majority of the works will be completed by the middle of October when the Store will once again be free of disruption.

Thank you once again for your letter.

Yours sincerely

Sandra Morris-Coole (Mrs)
Group Manager Customer Services

5

What *Not* To Do

English people are not, on the whole, naturally loud and aggressive. This is demonstrated by the fact that we have a remarkable propensity to apologize even when we have nothing to apologize about. This diffidence also manifests itself in an unwillingness to complain. Many people who steel themselves to register their disapproval about a particular issue go about complaining in the wrong way. Pitfalls to avoid include the following:

• Do not bother complaining to the Queen. Her hair dryer is also a bit temperamental. Poor old Mrs Windsor has got more than enough on her plate at the moment... her children, her hair dryer, the Commonwealth. A letter to Her Majesty will at best elicit a one liner from her private secretary or at worst will be ignored.

• Although it is generally a good idea to send an offending item to the managing director, used nappies are the exception to the rule. It is a criminal offence to send a noxious thing via the Royal Mail. I once had a problem with Tesco's own brand nappies and was sorely tempted to dispatch soiled examples to the company for laboratory analysis. The prospect of a weekend break at Pentonville even had its attractions but I eventually restrained myself.

• Do not fear those in authority. It is a conditioned reflex with most people to believe that letters written on important-looking headed notepaper or information generated by computers must be right. Not so. You should believe no one and accept nothing. My bank once wrote to me explaining that due to an error they had incorrectly credited my account with £100. Although this proved to be true I decided to deal with them as they would normally deal with me. I sent them a cheque for £90 and explained that I had deducted £10 in respect of my administrative charges. I heard no more. I am not a number. I am a free man.

• Do not behave like a wimp. You must instil a sense of fear into the opposition if your complaint is to succeed. I recall an incident at the reception desk at Center Parcs some time ago. An aggrieved father had been messed around to the point of torture over a high chair which he had paid for but not been given. His bottom line was to tell the receptionist that in his view, after three days without a high chair, the matter 'was moving towards a refund situation'. This feeble approach doubtless produced an equally feeble response. Needless to say, I was in the queue behind the man, waiting to ask the receptionist for the name of the company's chairman.

It is always good to build into a letter of complaint a series of tricky questions which put the managing director on the spot. Do these things often go wrong? Why did no one reply to my original letter? Who scored the opening goal in the 1967 FA Cup Final?

1 Virginia Street, London E1 9XP. Telephone: 071-782 4000. Telex: 262135.

Sir Peter Imbert
Commissioner
Metropolitan Police Force
London SW1H 0BG

25th November 1993

Dear Sir Peter

Emergence/ Emergency!

I am the Sun Newspaper's official complainer and I write on behalf of a Mr T Altay.

Mr Altay's problem is that he was given a parking ticket (ref:E765 BEV/001/ CG5/2JP) after parking on a yellow line outside Kings College Hospital on 4th October 1993. When he complained he was told that the fact that his wife was in labour (her waters had in fact broken) did not 'justify withdrawal of the fixed penalty'.

Please let me know whether or not the following events would 'justify withdrawal':-

1.   An invasion of martians.

2.   The coming of the Messiah.

3.   An earthquake recording 8 on the Richter Scale.

4.   The traffic warden in question having been diagnosed as a catatonic zombie.

5.   England qualifying for the World Cup on a technicality.

In all the circumstances I would be grateful if you would demonstrate to the Altay's new arrival that the British police still retain a spark of humanity.

I await your earliest reply.

Yours sincerely

Jasper Griegson

METROPOLITAN POLICE SERVICE

Central Ticket Office
P.O. Box 510
London SW1V 2JP

Dear Mr Griegson

FIXED PENALTY NOTICE NMC9767D

I refer to your letters dated 25 November and 5 December addressed to the Commissioner which have been passed to this office as the matters raised fall within my sphere of responsibility.

Whilst your comments are appreciated,I should explain that in this case Mr Altay chose to park on a busy main road despite the availability of parking spaces within Kings College Hospital. He left no explanation regarding his whereabouts and presumably left his vehicle illegally parked for the rest of the morning, thereby causing further inconvenience to those attending the hospital.

Whilst I am sympathetic to the situation,Mr Altay was clearly aware of the likely outcome of his actions and should not expect a dispensation unavailable to other, more considerate, expectant fathers.

In the circumstances I regret I am unable to alter the decision already conveyed to Mr Altay and suggest that he requests a court hearing if he wishes to pursue this matter.

Yours sincerely

A Johnson
for Officer in Charge

When you are a three-year-old boy and your Corgi toy garage falls apart, your world falls apart with it. The Polaris pen of an adult can remedy matters.

1 Virginia Street, London E1 9XP. Telephone: 071-782 4000. Telex: 262135.

7th January 1994

The Managing Director
Corgi Sales Limited
Leicester

Dear Sir

I am the Sun Newspaper's Official Complainer and I write on behalf of a Mrs L Baum.

Unlike me, Mrs Baum is not disposed to complain. Unfortunately however, your company has forced Mrs Baum to contact me with a view to resolving her problem.

On 22nd December Mrs Baum parted company with £35.17. She did so with a view to acquiring a working version of your 'Auto-City Super Electronic Garage' (hereinafter referred to as the 'Duff Toy') for her son. In short, the spiral car park element is so unstable that it would have been better used as a prop in the film Earthquake. Last time Mrs Baum attempted to construct the Duff Toy it recorded 7 on the Richter Scale. If you would like to being a seismograph to Harrow Weald Mrs Baum will happily given you a demonstration.

Other parts of the Duff Toy are equally shaky. If this were a microcosmic version of a real garage millions of pounds would have been lost and lives would have been put at risk. Fortunately this is not the cause.

Please compensate Mrs Baum's son without ado.

I trust that your personal intervention in this saga will bring it to a swift and mutually happy conclusion. Let me assure you now that a dismissive (but polite) two-line apology from your Customer Services Department will not suffice.

I await your prompt response.

Yours faithfully

Jasper Griegon

Corgi Toys
Meridian West
Leicester LE3 2WT

Telephone: 0533 826666
Fax: 0533 826640
Telex: 341856

A division of Mattel

CG/JM

11th January 1994

Dear Mr Griegson

Thank you for your letter. I was dismayed to read of Mrs Baum's son's disappointment with our Garage.

We are very jealous of our reputation as a manufacturer of quality products - this Garage has been in our range for three years, we have sold many hundreds of thousands of pieces of it around the world and I assure you that we would not have been able to do so if it was not a quality product.

However, as you and Mrs Baum will no doubt appreciate, in a mass production run the odd problem product is bound to slip through and I can only assume that there was a moulding problem in one or more of the components in this case. Without seeing the toy itself it is impossible to be more specific.

Nevertheless it is our policy in cases like this to recompense the consumer in full and I have sent a cheque for £35.17 to Mrs Baum. I have also enclosed a model to make up for the disappointment of her son and hopefully restore her and his opinion of Corgi. I enclose a copy of the letter.

Finally, let me thank you for bringing this problem to our attention. Let me reassure you that we have no plans to build fully-sized garages for NCP!

Yours sincerely

Chris Guest
Managing Director

It has now been 24 years since we last had a White Christmas in London. Working on the basis that there is one celestial managing director to whom even I cannot write, I decided to opt for the next best thing by complaining to the Meteorological Office.

1 Virginia Street, London E1 9XP. Telephone: 071-782 4000. Telex: 262135.

7th December 1993

Dr P. Ryder
Director of Operations
Meterological Office
London Road
Bracknell
Berks RG12 2SZ

Dear Dr Ryder

Re: Black Christmas

I am the Sun Newspaper's official complainer and I write on behalf of a large number of our readers who have expressed deep consternation concerning the following matter.

The problem in essence is that (1) every traditional Christmas card is littered with snow (2) the best selling record ever is "White Christmas" and (3) Christmas has become inseparable from images of snowballs, snowmen and snowflakes. Despite these facts the harsh reality is that we have not had a White Christmas in London since 1970.

I don't care how you do it but would you please arrange for a White Christmas this year. I can only assume that by a combination of 1990's high tech wizardry and the pulling of a few strings in high places you are able to achieve such things. Given that I have a personal financial interest in this matter (William Hill gave me excellent odds) I would be particularly grateful for a snowy Christmas day.

Unless I hear from you to the contrary I will assume that all is in hand.

Yours faithfully

J. Griege

Jasper Griegson

Director of Operations
Dr P. Ryder

Meteorological Office

London Road, Bracknell, Berkshire RG12 2SZ
United Kingdom
Telex: 849801
Tel: 0344 854608   Fax: 0344 856909

15 December 1993

Dear Mr Gregson,

CHRISTMAS — WHITE OR BLACK?

Thank you for writing to me on this matter. I have considered how best to respond — and decided not to suggest that the chance of a white Christmas would be much enhanced if the 'Sun' did not appear, nor to point out to you that some of your readers in this country and many prospective readers in Europe will have a white Christmas; noting that the world does not end at the outskirts of London, and quite a bit of the stuff is lying around in Scotland and the high ground in England, Wales and Northern Ireland.

It seemed much more appropriate to assist you in your financial dealings with William Hill by drawing your attention to the enclosed Christmas card. You will notice that this is not 'littered with snow' but imparts the useful information that in each of the last 9 years the maximum temperature in London on Christmas Day has been well above freezing. Therefore you will need very good odds indeed from William Hill and to take the long view if you are to gain from the exercise.

Of course, you should assume that those odds will have been calculated on the basis of information supplied by us. What you must try to do is get some 'up to date form' during the next few days, as Christmas Day begins to fall within the span of our forecasting ability. That will require a further small investment and a call to the London Weather Centre on 071-696-0573 or our Weathercall service on 0891 500 400, to obtain a 5-day forecast. Suffice to note that, at this stage we are expecting the amount of precipitation to be above average, and the temperature to be about average in South-East England over the Christmas period, which means that I have my money invested in William Hill's shares.

Whatever the weather, have a safe and enjoyable Christmas, with the best wishes of the Met Office.

Yours

P. Ryder

Some people take the view that, economic policies aside, what this country needs is a really unpleasant and protracted war against the French. This appeared to be an attitude held by a large insurance company. In the name of the oppressed Gallic people I decided to help.

1 Virginia Street, London E1 9XP. Telephone: 071-782 4000. Telex: 262135.

29 December 1993

C Johnston Esq.
Managing Director
Halifax Insurance plc
Halifax
West Yorkshire

Dear Mr Johnston

I am the Sun Newspaper's Official Complainer and I write on behalf of one of our most avid readers, Mr C Arnander.

As you know, Mr Arnander has a car insurance policy with your company. You have refused Mr Arnander permission to join on to his policy a friend, Ms F Gourlet. Your justification for this refusal is that Ms Gourlet is French. Surely the time has come to put the past behind us.

    We stuffed the French at Agincourt

    We thrashed them again at Trafalgar and Waterloo

    Most important of all we trounced them in the 1982 World Cup - do you remember that stunning strike by Bryan Robson?

We all know that given half a chance your average Englishman would would happily spearhead a thousand bomber raid on Paris tomorrow but the time must come when enough is enough (or un oeuf is un oeuf as they say over there).

Notwithstanding your xenophobia I appeal to the speck of Francophilia which may possibly be lurking within you and ask you to reconsider. I await your earliest reply.

Yours sincerely

J. Griegson

Jasper Griegson

Halifax
INSURANCE PLC

7 January 1994

Dear Monsieur Griegson

I refer to your letter of 29 December 1993 regarding your avid reader Mr Arnander and note your comments about the French.

Whilst at school I actually enjoyed French, we had an excellent teacher, a Monsieur Griegson - it's not you is it? If so I promise to return the text books forthwith! The same school as Gordon Kaye I would add.

So, I personally have no hang ups about the French, or the Germans for that matter, and am glad to report that Mr Arnander's problem, if you can call the lovely Ms Gourlet a problem (she sounds delicious to me), was actually resolved on the day of your letter, with Ms Gourlet being added to the policy during her short visit to this country.

I do hope that you are assured that Halifax Insurance is not xenophobic and is a caring insurer, especially with the ladies - a copy of promotional literature (enclosed) proves the point. No doubt you'll be able to inform your readers of these simple facts.

Yours sincerely

Monsieur Christopher Johnstone
Managing Director

6

Some Golden Rules

The golden rule is of course that there are no golden rules. You should treat an irritating grievance as a wonderful opportunity to assert and express yourself with no holds barred. If there is a guiding principle it is this: *Go for it.*

- There is no reason to limit yourself to one letter of complaint if five identical letters to people in authority might improve matters. I once wrote an identical letter to three different directors of Dixons regarding a faulty stereo. The first told me to go to hell, the second offered me ten per cent off my next purchase, the third provided a full refund! Do not assume that high-powered directors of large companies talk to each other. Of course they don't. The great myth about the senior management of any large company is that it exists at all.

- Abuse is generally unproductive. To engage in an unseemly rant is to condescend to the level of banging fists on tables. This normally achieves nothing. Alitalia were less than impressed when I once sent them a volley of invective coupled with a sick bag.

• A typed letter is usually better than a composition comprising of spidery scrawl. If the reader must first plough his or her way through a mire of hieroglyphics they are far less likely to be sympathetic to your cause.

• Equally, short is sweet. One page of drivel is infinitely better than seventeen pages of drivel. Ask any examination marker. A skilful complainer will always go straight for the jugular by means of a short, sharp dispatch. A voluminous treatise is rarely called for.

• Fear no one. For the price of a postage stamp you are free to communicate with anyone you like – the chairman of ICI, the managing director of Volkswagen, the Secretary of State for the Environment...the list is endless. They are all waiting for a really interesting letter. Most of their morning post is desperately uninteresting. Make their day. Make your day too. The envelopes on your door mat will not just be of the nasty brown variety.

I once appeared on Radio 4. I complained about the programme to the Broadcasting Complaints Commission. Not only did they take my complaint to heart, they telephoned me at home to quiz me about the seriousness of my problem. I told them that I was not serious at all. They were very upset indeed and put the phone down on me. This was a refreshing reminder that some Great British Institutions are still run by people who have not smiled since 1952.

Canon P Pilkington
Chairman
The Broadcasting Complaints Commission
Grosvenor Gardens House
35-37 Grosvenor Gardens
London SW1W OBS

Dear Cannon

"Tuesday Live" - 16th February 1993

I wish to register a complaint of the most serious kind.

In 1960 Andy Warhol said:-

    "In the future, everyone will be famous for 15 minutes".

I am due to appear on the above-mentioned Radio 4 programme concerning the art of complaining. I have been told however that despite having been interviewed for 1½ hours, I will only appear for a maximum of 9 minutes. In other words, the BBC are short changing me out of 6 minutes and I would like to know why. I look to you for substantial and wholly unwarranted compensation. If you listen into the programme you will realise that I can easily be bought off with two bars of Cadbury's chocolate.

I await your earliest response.

Yours sincerely

Jasper Griegson

cc   N Trevethick Esq
       BBC

The Broadcasting Complaints Commission

Grosvenor Gardens House
35 & 37 Grosvenor Gardens
London SW1W 0BS

Telephone: 071 630 1966

R.D. HEWLETT
SECRETARY

16 February 1993

Dear Mr Griegson,

Thank you for your recent, undated letter about today's edition of *Tuesday Lives* on BBC Radio 4. The Chairman has asked me to reply.

The function of the Commission is to consider and adjudicate upon complaints of unjust or unfair treatment in broadcast programmes and complaints of unwarranted infringement of privacy in, or in connection with, such programmes. The Commission cannot require a broadcaster to compensate a complainant; the only sanction available to them is a direction that the broadcaster publish a summary of their adjudication upon a complaint.

If, having listened to this programme, you believe that you were unjustly or unfairly treated in it, please would you complete and return the enclosed form. The enclosed guidance leaflet gives further information about the Commission's remit and procedures.

Yours sincerely,

C. D. Howells

Enc   C D HOWELLS

The Broadcasting Complaints Commission

Grosvenor Gardens House
35 & 37 Grosvenor Gardens
London SW1W OBS

Telephone: 071 630 1966

R.D. HEWLETT
SECRETARY

8 March 1993

Dear Mr Griegson,

Tuesday Lives, BBC Radio 4, 16 February 1993

I am sorry for the delay in acknowledging receipt of your complaint form.

I will place your complaint before the Commission at their meeting on Wednesday and will write to you again afterwards.

Yours sincerely,

R D HEWLETT

The comic singer-songwriter Jake Thackray once philosophized about human beings in authority with the following words: 'The bigger the bull, the bigger the bullshite falls.' This is true. In some cases literally.

1 Virginia Street, London E1 9XP. Telephone: 071-782 4000. Telex: 262135.

A. Wood Esq
Chief Executive
Brent Borough Council
Wembley

Dear Mr Wood

I am the Sun Newspaper's Official Complainer and I write on behalf of a group of our readers who are concerned that your borough is failing to comply with its statutory obligations concerning the environment.

The problem in question is very unpleasant indeed but in order for you to really understand it, it is necessary for you put down this letter and go immediately to the junction between Shoot Up Hill and Christchurch Avenue in Kilburn where you will find a railway bridge. Stand under the bridge for ten minutes or so with this letter in your hands and then move on to the next paragraph.

Good. That's better.

By now you will have been bombed with pigeon shit. Moreover you will have noticed that the pavement is totally unsafe for the old and infirm since it is, not surprisingly, smothered in excrement from the source above your head. When wet, the surface of the pavement becomes a slippery cross-breed between an ice rink and a toilet. One of our readers spends, for obvious reasons, a substantial part of his disposable income on dry cleaning bills. This intolerable situation could easily be remedied by the use of nets under the bridge which would prevent this ornithological squadron of the Luftwaffe from perching on the rafters.

Unless I hear from you to the contrary I will assume:- (a) that you will have remedied this problem by next Monday or (b) that you authorise me to have nets installed at the Council's expense and\or (c) that I am instructed to give Shoot Up Hill a good reason for calling itself by that name.

Yours sincerely

Jasper Griegson

THE CHIEF
EXECUTIVE'S OFFICE

CHARLES WOOD, CHIEF EXECUTIVE

YOUR REF.
OUR REF.

YOUR CONTACT
TELEPHONE

PRESS AND PUBLICITY,
ROOM 3, BRENT TOWN HALL,
FORTY LANE, WEMBLEY,
MIDDLESEX HA9 9HX.
TEL. 081-908 7050.
FAX 081-908 7166.

1 February 1994

Dear Mr Griegson

I hope you won't think ill
Of this response, re: Shoot-up-Hill

I certainly cannot deny
The lateness of this humble reply

Your letter about the pigeon shit
Was, with us, an immediate hit

Our team have already cleared the mess
And all that terrible unpleasantness

We cannot, however, put up the netting
The point at which, I think, you're getting

The bridge, you see, is not ours to fix,
Although we've cleaned the visible bricks

It belongs to a bit of British Rail
Upon whose efforts we will prevail

To find a longer term solution
To prevent the environmental pollution

The Luftwaffe were seen off by British pluck
I'm sure that with a little luck

And I can assure this is truely meant
We will help stop the excrement

From adding to the cleaning bill
Of local residents of Shoot-up-Hill

Responses like this must be the bane 'a
People who are titled Official Complainer

But you see, Jasper, old fruit
From now your correspondent's suit

Will be as clean as a whistle
And so ends this short epistle.

John Walker
Chief Public Relations Officer

press ✚ publicity

1 Virginia Street, London E1 9XP. Telephone: 071-782 4000. Telex: 262135.

4th February 1994

John Walker Esq
Chief Public Relations Officer
Brent Council
Wembley

Dear Mr Walker

Thank you for your excellent letter of 1st February. Naturally
I felt compelled to respond.

Yours sincerely

J. Griege

Jasper Griegson

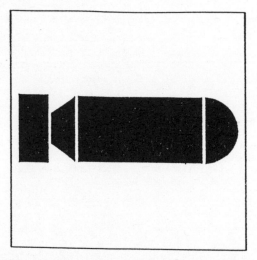

RE: BIRD BOMBING AT SHOOT UP HILL

Thanks for the poem, but I'm still not happy

The road and pavements are still quite

crappy!

THE CHIEF
EXECUTIVE'S OFFICE

CHARLES WOOD, CHIEF EXECUTIVE

YOUR REF.
OUR REF.

YOUR CONTACT
TELEPHONE

PRESS AND PUBLICITY,
ROOM 3, BRENT TOWN HALL,
FORTY LANE, WEMBLEY,
MIDDLESEX HA9 9HX.
TEL. 081-908 7050.
FAX 081-908 7166.

Dear Mr Griegson

25 February 1994

The job is done,
The crap is gone.

We are pressing
To get the netting

Put in place
Under the space

Where pigeons crap
And cause mishap.

British Rail are the crew
Who really must do

What is desired
and certainly required

To stop the nesting
And pigeon infesting.

Until they erect
The wretched net,

We'll foot the bill
To clean Shoot-Up-Hill

Once every week.
We'll even seek

To truly ensure
Complaints no more,

By sending snoops,
To scoop the poops,

Not simply meekly,
But certainly weekly.

John Walker
Chief Public Relations Officer

press + publicity

I was once libelled by Woman *magazine. Needless to say I was overjoyed. I suppose that the pleasure I received must be akin to that of a masochist who is offered a powdered glass sandwich and a pint of bleach to wash it down. The* Independent *newspaper also had a crack. If anyone else wishes to defame me please go ahead. Make my day.*

The News Editor
The Independent
40 City Road
London
EC1Y 2DB

31st March 1988

Dear Sir

I write to complain in the strongest possible terms about the
large photograph which dominated the front page of the edition of
your newspaper dated Friday 25th March. I register my complaint
in the alternative:-

1.   I am featured in the photograph but I am decidedly out of
      focus. This fact undoubtedly dissipated the happiness my
      mum might otherwise have had upon seeing the fruit of her
      loins splashed across a national newspaper. Surely your
      cameraman could have taken a better snap of me.

      OR

2.   The text accompanying the said photograph fails to make it
      clear that the 'animal' referred to is the man on the left,
      rather than the man on the right. The members of the
      football team that I play for often refer to me as an
      animal by way of compliment. I didn't nick £13,000,000.
      Please publish an apology.

Yours sincerely

J. Griegson

Jasper Griegson

NEWSPAPER PUBLISHING PLC
40 City Road, London EC1Y 2DB
Telephone: 01-253 1222 Telex: 9419611
Fax: 01-608 1552, 01-608 1149 (Editorial only)

8th April 1988

Dear Mr Griegson

Thank you for your letter passed to me from the News Editor. I have noted the complaints ...

1.   Regrettably the photographer failed to grasp the whole point of the story and instead of focussing on a bystander decided to train his lens on the man that the story was about and I will reprimand him.

2.   I really feel that even though your image is in soft focus it is sufficiently evident that you have no resemblance to an animal.

Thank you for your picture we will keep it on file for use on the next occasion when you happen to be on the periphery of a news event.

Yours sincerely

Alan John
PICTURE EDITOR

an await Guinness trial in California

7

Trivial Disputes

Human beings are sensitive creatures. A tiny stone in your shoe can be enormously upsetting. Similarly, if you have spent 21 pence on a packet of crisps only to discover that the contents are moist, the sense of indignation can be immense. Once you have realized that the best way to deal with such minor irritations is to enjoy them, life becomes much more pleasurable. There is nothing so small that it is not worthy of a complaint, once you appreciate that complaining can be an end in itself.

I once pursued a complaint against British Rail concerning a piece of toast. My wife was travelling first class on an early morning Pullman to Manchester. She fancied a piece of toast. The jobsworth waiter told her that notwithstanding the copious quantities of toast on the tray he was holding, he was not allowed to give her a slice. From the point of view of British Rail there was of course a reason for this. The customer is not always right. My wife was informed that she had to have a full English breakfast (inclusive of toast) or alternatively could go to the buffet and buy a toasted sandwich. She wanted neither of these things. She simply wanted a piece of toast. After a welter of correspondence British Rail eventually made a change to their Pullman advertisement. There was a great feeling of satisfaction in having caused them huge aggravation but what they didn't know was that if they had posted me a slice of toast after my first letter I would have been more than happy.

I also had a run in with London Zoo over an ant. The Zoo operates a scheme whereby members of the public can adopt a creature for a year and thus contribute to its upkeep. Adopting a tiger can cost thousands of pounds. The minimum charge for small animals used to be £15. A friend of mine, whose miserliness knows no boundaries, was getting married. I decided that a fitting wedding present would be for me to adopt an ant for him and his bride. I categorically informed London Zoo that I wanted an ordinary ant. I did not want an expensive, top-of-the-range ant. After I had parted company with my £15 I received a certificate duly appointing my friend and his wife to be the

adoptive parents of Arthur the Ant. Needless to say, Arthur turned out not to be an ordinary ant at all, but rather a flashy variety of wood ant. Imagine my horror. I took up the matter with the Zoo, adding to my original gripe that Arthur would never, in the course of his somewhat limited lifespan, be able to munch his way through £15 worth of food. Sadly, the relevant officials in charge of the adopt-an-animal scheme had had their sense of humour surgically removed at birth and never responded to my letters. I toyed with the idea of trying to make Arthur a ward of court but never quite got around to it. A rare defeat.

The Person in Charge of Adopted Animals
London Zoo
Regents Park
London W1

9th February 1988

Dear Sir

I enclose for your urgent attention a picture of my adopted leopard shark (hereinafter referred to as 'Cyril'). Having recently visited Cyril at his mock reconstruction of the Pacific Ocean on your premises I noticed that he looked decidedly off colour.

I would be most grateful if you would let me know whether or not, in the event of his demise, I might be able to take possession of Cyril's body with a view to stuffing it. I assume that as a proud parent I have every right to do this and if I do not hear from you to the contrary I will assume this arrangement is acceptable.

In any event, I would much prefer it if Cyril lives. It may be that a better diet would improve matters. How about some human flesh?

I look forward to your earliest reply.

Yours sincerely

Jasper Griegson

There are few things more distressing in life than a spider in the bath. A black bit in your bowl of cereal, however, runs a close second.

```
The Customer Relations Manager
Grocers Supply Limited
80b Cricklewood Broadway
London
NW2 3ED
```

19th Auguste 1987

Dear Sir,
        In the Matter of a rogue Cocoa Puffe

Thus it came to passe that I wak'd fromme my nightly Slumber. Possess'd of a weaknesse withinne me for a Bowle of Cocoa Puffes I crep'd tyr'd and hungry in my Nakednesse t'ward the Kitchinn whence I retriev'd the saide foodstuffe fromme the larder. I pour'd my Bowle to the brimme and humbly sat upon my breakfaste Stool to purtake of the Cereal. As I ate my Eye cawte syte of a Surprize. Not Cocoa Puffes at all but ungodly bullette-shap'd Thinges. I enclose one for your attention.
Pleaze let me knowe how this Abomination came into Being.
I beg to remaine Your Honourable Servant

J. Grieper

90

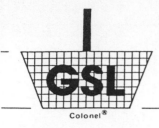

Colonel®

GROCERS SUPPLY LIMITED

34 Ashford Court Ashford Road London NW2 6BW
Telephone 01-208 0755/2588   Telex 938047 GRSPLY G   Fax 01-452 6212

FOOD SERVICE DIVISION • GROCERY DIVISION • HEALTH & BEAUTY PRODUCTS

21st August 1987

Dear Mr Griegson

What superb style. I really enjoyed your letter although I am
sorry that it had to be as a result of a complaint. I would have
responded in similar rhetoric, but felt the issue deserved a
slightly more serious approach from us.

Enormous care is taken in the U S A factories, where our supplies
are packed, however, there is always the 'Rogue' that slips the
net, and it would seem that you were unfortunate enough to be the
recipient. For this I do apologize, and greatly appreciate the
light hearted approach you have adopted.

I am sending you under separate cover, a replacement box of your
cereal, together with a box of the latest cereal, so new that we
have not even finalised the packaging yet. I am also sending you
a 'Cheerios' Tea shirt for your use. I tried to trace you on the
telephone to check your size, but could obtain no listing for
you. I hope I was right in my size assumption.

Finally, thank you for your support for General Mills Products,
support that we value enormously.

Yours sincerely

Paul P Vegoda

ipcmagazines

David Sainsbury
Chairman
J Sainsbury plc
Stamford Street
London SE1 9LL

27 June 1994

Dear Mr Sainsbury

I am Woman's Realm Magazine's Official Complainer and I write on behalf of a Mrs S Style.

Neither Mrs Style nor I mean to be picky but the enclosed tweezers purchased at one of your stores suffer from the following defect:

They don't work.

Mrs Style parted company with the princely sum of 69 pence on the following apparently false assumption:

They would work.

Well they don't and Mrs Style is very upset. She bought the tweezers in the hope of expunging some unsightly hair from areas of Mr Style's body where hair growth is anything but desirable and certainly not normal. As a consequence Mrs Style remains married to an unplucked hirsute husband whose orang-utang appearance is starting to cause some consternation at his office.

Please intervene but make it snappy. London Zoo have already expressed interest.

Yours sincerely

Jasper Griegson

29 July 1994

Dear Mrs Style

We have been contacted by Jasper Greigson of Woman's
Realm about your complaint. I am sorry that you have
found our tweezers to be unsatisfactory.

It is our intention that all our products are offered for
sale in perfect condition and they are tested to ensure
that they are suitable for the purpose intended before
being introduced sale in our stores.

This particular product comes to us from a reputable
supplier and continues to sell well in our stores. We
have not received any other complaints but in view of
your experience, my buyers will ensure that the tweezers
are retested and that they meet with our requirements.

I would like you to have the enclosed voucher to
reimburse your expenses and I hope that you will not be
deterred from shopping at Sainsbury's.

Yours sincerely

M Rosen
Director of Grocery Buying

Enc: £5 Voucher

A work colleague of mine used to complain to me week after week about the TV cop Bergerac. Her problem was not with Jim Bergerac himself (whom she clearly rather fancied) but with Jim's stroppy girlfriend who did nothing but moan when Jim went off to do battle with the criminals of Jersey. Amazingly, a few weeks after I wrote to complain, Jim's girlfriend was written out of the series by being murdered. My colleague still believes to this day that I harbour supernatural powers.

The Director General
The British Broadcasting Corporation
Wood Lane
London
W12 8QT

3rd March 1988

Dear Sir

Re Bergerac's Girlfriend

I write as a keen and regular viewer of your excellent television programme Bergerac. I must say that I am sad to see that the current series has ended but I wait with bated breath for the next one.

Despite the overall high quality of the drama I feel that now is the appropriate time to lodge a formal complaint against the character of Bergerac's girlfriend. The said female can only be described as a plain, sullen, miserable, swivel-eyed yuppie and I would be most grateful if you could arrange for her to be deleted from all future episodes. She really is a hideous bitch and my guess is that Jim too must be sick and tired of her depressing whinging.

I look forward to hearing from you with a copy of her dismissal notice.

Yours faithfully

Jasper Griegson

BBC

BRITISH BROADCASTING CORPORATION
BROADCASTING HOUSE LONDON W1A 1AA
TELEPHONE 01-580 4468   TELEX: 265781
TELEGRAMS AND CABLES: BROADCASTS LONDON TELEX

Dear Mr Griegson

I have been asked to thank you for your letter, addressed to the Director-General, received here on 10th March.

I must explain that the Director-General receives a vast amount of correspondence and cannot undertake to reply personally to everyone. Please be assured, though, that your interest in 'Bergerac' was appreciated and that the comments and points of view you express have been brought to the notice of the producer responsible for this series.

Yours sincerely

Jane Barrow
Programme Correspondence

C Hedges Esq
Managing Director
United International Pictures (UK) Ltd
37 Mortimer Street
London W1   21st September 1993

Dear Mr Hedges

<u>"Jurassic Park"</u>

Two weeks ago I went to see the above-mentioned film at a cinema in Staples Corner,
London a film which I understand your company distributes. I paid £3.80 for my ticket but
encountered a problem. I looked under my seat. It wasn't there. I asked at the sweet shop
in the foyer. It wasn't there. I went to the gents but it wasn't there either. In fact it was
simply nowhere to be found anywhere in the cinema. What, you may ask was I looking for?
The plot.

I would be most grateful indeed if you would refund me the £3.80 which I appear to have
wasted.

Yours sincerely

J. Griegson

<u>Jasper Griegson</u>

p.s   I would mention by way of mitigation that I thought that "Raiders" and "Jaws" were
        excellent. At least they had a storyline.

The Manager
The Odeon Cinema
Leicester Square
London
W1

23rd July 1987

Dear Sir

I write to express my deep disenchantment at the execrable
service suffered by my fiancee and I in the course of a recent
visitation to your noble establishment. Upon our arrival we both
felt a trifle parched in the throat and accordingly decided to
partake of two of your bumper-sized seventy pence cups of Coca
Cola. Far from quenching our immense thirst, the beverage
supplied to us was completely flat. It was little more than
zestless brown slop and expensive brown slop at that. I
registered my displeasure with the refreshment executives serving
behind the confectionary counter who reposted thus:-
'Sorry mate but that's all there is.' I realised at that stage
that I was up against intellectual giants. My attempts to obtain
a financial reinstatement in exchange for a return of the noxious
draft failed.

I enclose two tickets and one of the said vessels as proof of
purchase. Kindly restore my faith in your staff, your cinema and
the notion of good customer relations.

Your Obedient Servant

J. Griegson

Jasper Griegson

With the compliments of

ODEON

Dear Mr Griegson

Many thanks for your letter dated the 23rd
instant. I regret the incident which took place.
I will be investigating the same. Please have
faith in the 'Odeon' and please accept my guest
tickets to be taken to the next presentation.

Odeon Theatre Leicester Square London WC2H 7LQ Telephone 01 930 6111/4

Although I criticize most organizations, there is one body whose integrity is unimpeachable: International Rescue. Let no man take the name of Thunderbirds in vain.

Tony the Tiger
c/o T A Knowlton Esq
Chairman and Managing Director
Kelloggs Company of Great Britain Ltd
Manchester
M16 0PU

20th October 1992

Dear Tony

Re: Television Advertisement - Thunderbirds

I wish to complain in the strongest possible terms about your television advertisement involving Kelloggs Frosties. I represent the Tracey family and I was most disturbed indeed to note that in the course of the advertisement you are shown hurling Thunderbirds 2 and 3 through the air as though they were mere 'toys'. This activity is certainly not G-R-E-A-T!

I would like to remind you that the structure of both these aircraft is extremely sensitive and that by improper handling you may well damage the paintwork or worse still the bodywork. If these Thunderbirds were to be put out of action thousands of lives could be put at risk. In these circumstances, I look to you for written confirmation that you will desist from this outrageous behaviour and by way of compensation I sincerely hope that you will send (care of my house) a year's supply of free Frosties for the entire Tracey family.

Unless I hear from you to the contrary, within five working days, I will have no option but to advise Jeff Tracey and the boys to give up eating Frosties altogether.

I look forward to receiving your urgent response.

Yours sincerely

Jasper Griegson

Kellogg's

KELLOGG COMPANY OF GREAT BRITAIN LIMITED

The Kellogg Building, Talbot Road, Manchester, M16 0PU. Telephone: 061-869 2000 Telex: 667031 Fax: 061-869 2100

By appointment to
HM The Queen,
Purveyors of Cereals,
Kellogg Company of Great Britain Ltd.
Manchester

2nd November 1992

Dear Jasper

KELLOGG'S FROSTIES - THUNDERBIRDS PROMOTION

Thank you for your recent letter to Tony the Tiger. We were concerned to learn of your distress regarding Tony's use of Thunderbirds 2 and 3. As I am sure you are aware Tony is not prone to unruly or anti-social behaviour. Moreover he would never harm a member or associate of the Thunderbirds team.

We would understand your distress had the items in question been the Thunderbirds 2 and 3. In fact these items are devilishly clever replica models. Tony thinks this promotion is indeed G-R-E-A-T because with these unique toys children can have even more fun with Thunderbirds. Only putting them aside when Jeff Tracey and the boys are on the box.

Yours sincerely

S M George
Senior Brand Manager

9th October 1992

The Managing Director
Nestle Holdings (UK) Plc
St George's House
Croydon
Surrey CR9 1NR

Dear Sirs

THUNDERBIRDS - KITKATS

I wish to register a complaint of the most serious kind.

I represent Jeff Tracey and his sons, Scott, Virgil, Alan, Gordon
and John. Last night whilst watching my television I saw your
latest advertisement for Kitkats. As you are well aware (and I
am sure you take personal responsibility for this) the
advertisment depicted Scott in Thunderbird 1 sitting with his
feet up eating a Kitkat. We all know that in truth Scott
dedicates his time to helping people and fending off the Hood.
This is a disgraceful defamation of my client and I have advised
him that unless within the next 24 hours, he receives a lorry
load of Kitkats for himself and for the other members of
International Rescue (not forgetting Lady Penelope, Parker, Tin
Tin, Brains and Grandma!)(via my house where they occasionally
reside) he will have no option but to commence libel proceedings
against you without further notice.

International Rescue is an organisation committed to helping
people and the fact that you have distorted its image for
commercial gain hardly befits your company. I look forward to
receiving a personal apology (in kind) from you and I trust that
you will treat this letter with the seriousness which it
deserves.

Yours faithfully

J. Griegson

Jasper 'Having a break' Griegson

Nestlé UK Ltd
Nestlé Rowntree Division

YORK YO1 1XY

TELEPHONE (0904) 653071
TELEX 57846 ROWMAC G
FACSIMILE (0904) 622467

Dear Mr Griegson

Thunderbirds – Kit Kat

Thank you for your letter dated 9th October 1992, which the Chairman, Peter Blackburn, has asked me to deal with as a matter of urgency.

I am surprised that Jeff Tracey has not spoken to you about our Kit Kat commercial as he cooperated fully with its development and production.

I can reassure you that the commercial was filmed in between rescues and that International Rescue remained on standby at all times. No lives were put at risk as the result of this film.

I am sure you will appreciate that, at times, life on the island is a little quiet, and that the Tracey boys enjoy relaxing in a variety of ways. Given all the tremendous work that International Rescue do on behalf of all of us we cannot begrudge them a break every now and then. The filming was great fun and with everyone entering in to the spirit of things – even Parker raised a smile.

Scott is, of course, an avid fan of Kit Kat, and we have guaranteed an unlimited supply of product to him and his brothers, so that they can continue to enjoy their well deserved breaks from helping to save the world from evil and disaster. It is unlikely, therefore, that Scott will have any use for a further lorry load of Kit Kat as you have requested on his behalf in your letter.

Thank you for writing to us with your serious complaint. I trust that my explanation has put you at your ease and that you appreciate that we were not in anyway disgracing the good name of International Rescue. I understand however that your concerns are based on the very best of intentions and I have therefore arranged for a special delivery of Kit Kat to be made to you which I hope you will accept as a gift from Nestle Rowntree.

No strings attached.

Yours sincerely

D BOX
MARKETING

1st December 1987

The Managing Director
British Telecom plc
Holborn Viaduct
London

Dear Sir

I wish to complain about the whopping great faux pas which you
and your company have made in the choice of music for your latest
television commercial. I resent the use of the Thunderbirds
theme tune as a means of advancing your prestige and popularity.
International Rescue is an organisation dedicated to assisting
those in need with no regard whatever for profit motives. I find
it nothing short of scandalous that you have misappropriated the
Tracy family's melody for your own sinister ends. It is my
belief that you may well have been infiltrated by the evil HOOD,
in which case you would be well advised to winkle him out, give
him his P45 and send him packing. I enclose a photo for ease of
identification.

It may concern you to learn that Jeff Tracy has taken
professional advice on this matter and that you may well get a
writ any day now. As a gesture of solidarity it is my intention
to deduct 10% from all my future telephone bills until you drop
the Thunderbirds music. I will donate the sums to International
Rescue. Unless I hear from you to the contrary I will assume
this arrangement is acceptable to you.

I await your earliest response.

Yours faithfully

J. Griegson

Jasper Griegson

British
T'EL.ECOM

Corporate Relations   Telephone 01-356 5388

British Telecom Centre
81 Newgate Street
LONDON
EC1A 7AJ

8th January 1988

Dear Mr Griegson

Thank you for your letter of 1 December about our use of the
Thunderbirds music in one of our television commercials.

I am very sorry it has not been possible to reply sooner, but I
hope the enclosed will explain all!

Yours sincerely

RW Evans

R W EVANS
Head of Central
Advertising Services

Dear Mr Griegson

I have intercepted your letter. How did you find me out?

My disguise was perfect, my cover faultless.

And yet you, a humble subscriber have discovered the greatest, the most foolproof, the most devious plan yet, of The Hood.

Yes, curse you, I have indeed infiltrated the ranks of British Telecom.

With but one aim, the ultimate destruction of the accursed International Rescue Organisation.

As you shall not live to tell the tale, you shall hear of my plan.

I had learned months ago that British Telecom were going to call in that meddling goody goody Jeff Tracy and his impossibly handsome sons to help with their network modernisation.

So using all the cunning and guile at my command (a lot, as I'm sure you are aware my friend) I became part of the British Telecom Organisation.

I ensured I was there on the day when International Rescue, curse them, arrived at the Telecom Tower.

As the TV commercial cameras turned, my own carefully hidden lens recorded the secrets of those infernal machines, Thunderbirds One and Two.

You may recall that I have tried to take photographs of the Tracy equipment many times over the years but to no avail. This time, however, there would be no mistake!

(Note that the actual Thunderbirds were carefully edited out of the finished Telecom TV commercial for 'security reasons'. Hah! Those fools!)

But in my eagerness, I faltered. Once again I had reckoned without the deadly charm and fabulous good looks of International Rescue's British Agent, Lady Penelope Creighton-Ward.

While she held me enthralled at the base of the tower, her snivelling lackey Parker picked my pocket, spiriting away my precious film forever.

A plague on all your houses Jeff Tracy.   Not to mention your island.

Meanwhile British Telecom, in homage to International Rescue, have retained that ridiculous Thunderbirds theme (<u>not</u> in order to advance their prestige and popularity - Telecom wouldn't think of that).

But what is this?

You intend to donate 10% of your telephone subscription to International Rescue? My eyes light up with rage!

Are you mad?

You seek to undo years of work, decades of painstaking effort to bring International Rescue to its knees and myself to prominence as Master of the World.

British Telecom may find your gesture funny and clever (although they don't go along with it - hard luck) but I, The Hood, am far from amused.

Because I intend to stay here, invisible in British Telecom's underbelly, awaiting another chance to strike at Tracy and his angelic offspring.

Be forever silent and I may spare your miserable life.

Do not and .... well, I have your address.

Yours in fun,

The Hood

PS I'd like the negative of the picture you sent.

PPS No, I demand it!

    H

If you look at a £50 note (or indeed any other note) you will see the signature of a Mr Kentfield. He is a very nice man and an excellent ally if your complaint concerns issues of dosh. I enlisted his help to great effect.

1 Virginia Street, London E1 9XP. Telephone: 071-782 4000. Telex: 262135.

17th January 1993

David Bailey Esq
Managing Director
Travellers Fare Ltd
50 Paul Street
London EC2A 4AE

Re: Funny Money

I am the Sun Newspaper's official complainer and I write on behalf of a number of our readers who have expressed their profound concern about the following matter. A number of your Traveller's Fare restaurants do not, as a matter of strict policy, accept £50 notes.

I would like to understand what it is about Her Majesty's currency that you find so offensive. Is it the rather sickly colour of the paper? Is it that you do not accept legal tender and would prefer to be paid in brightly coloured beads? Or is it that you suspect that £50 notes are a bit dodgy and would prefer to handle wads of unmarked used fivers with non-sequential numbers?

When I drew this point to the attention of the Bank of England they registered extreme surprise (see letter attached).

Please enlighten our readers.

I thank you in advance for your assistance.

Yours sincerely

Jasper Griegson

cc. A.W. Jarvis Esq. General Manager, Printing Works, Bank of England

·TRAVELLERS·FARE·LIMITED·

20 January 1994

Dear Mr Griegson

Thank you for writing to me in your official complainer capacity and enclosing a letter from the heart of the banking world.

Notices, which advise customers that change cannot be given for £50 notes, should remain in only a very few of our units. Those that do remain are in places where having sufficient change on-hand, for a transaction of perhaps £1, could cause difficulties.

As your letter indicates that problems are still arising, I have reminded all staff that the Company does accept £50 notes, but I hope that you and your readers will agree that if change is not available, accepting the note is a not a practical proposition.

As to your suggestion that we "suspect £50 notes to be a bit dodgy", we have managed to steady our nerves by the introduction of note checking equipment, which provides a useful backup for our staff.

You may reassure your readers that we recognise genuine £50 notes as legal tender and you may also reassure Mr Kentfield that we consider his products excellent value and worth every penny.

Yours sincerely

D L BAILEY
MANAGING DIRECTOR

BANK OF ENGLAND
LONDON EC2R 8AH

G E A Kentfield
Chief of the Banking Department
and Chief Cashier
071-601 4361

30 December 1993

Dear Mr Griegson

The General Manager of the Printing Works has passed me your letter of 16 December. I found it intriguing. I would have expected any shop or restaurant to accept any current British banknote.   I am not aware of BRTF's reasons for rejecting £50 notes nor whether this is a general policy or a view taken by individual managers. If the reason is, for example, the amount of change they are willing to carry then that is a business matter and not something for us to comment upon.

Certainly I hope that the rejection - if that is what it is - does not reflect concern over the authenticity of the banknotes since this can be readily checked. Indeed we encourage everyone to check their banknotes since they are valuable bearer documents. Specific security features to look out for include the feel of the paper, the existence of a good quality watermark and windowed thread embedded in the paper as well as the quality of the colour and printing. Once familiar with genuine notes, as cashiers certainly would be, the first three checks that I have mentioned take only a few seconds and are the most reliable methods of verification. If any doubt remains, a few seconds more may be spent looking at the quality of the colour and printing of the note.   Most retail outlets are familiar with these features and have no difficulty with any of our notes.

Yours sincerely

G.E.A.Kentfield .

9th November 1993

The Managing Director
Nestle Holdings (UK) Plc
St George's House
Croydon
Surrey CR9 1NR

Dear Sir

As the Sun Newspaper's official complainer, I write on behalf of
one of our readers a Mr J Stock.

Mr Stock has passed to me the enclosed mutant smartie. As you
will see it appears to be a fusion of two blue smarties and is
probably best described as a confectionery form of siamese twin.
Since watching John Hurt's virtuoso performance in 'The Elephant
Man' I have never seen anything quite as hideous as this but I
would welcome your comments. Please let me know whether or not
your company has made a serious manufacturing error or whether it
is conducting some form of grotesque genetic experiment.

I look forward to seeing the laboratory report.

Yours faithfully

Jasper Griegson

Nestlé UK Ltd
Nestlé Rowntree Division

YORK, YO1 1XY.
TELEPHONE (0904) 653071
TELEX 57846 ROWMAC G
FACSIMILE (0904) 622467

17th November 1993

Dear Mr Stock

We were concerned to learn of your complaint from Mr Griegson about one of our products.

Examination has confirmed that the confectionery is defective due to a manufacturing fault and should have been rejected prior to packing. We suspect that during the manufacture process two Smarties have somehow fused together as one. We will be bringing this to the attention of the Production Manager concerned.

We would like to assure you that great care is taken during all stages of manufacture and packing in an attempt to ensure that our products reach our customers in good condition.

May we say how sorry we are that you have been disappointed by one of our products. We hope that you will be able to use the enclosed cheque to purchase some more confectionery and that this will go some way toward making up for what has happened.

Yours sincerely

Lesley Lee (Mrs)
Admin Head, Consumer Services

Enc cheque for £2.00

ipcmagazines

Sir Geoffrey Mulcahy
Chairman
Kingfisher plc
119 Marylebone Road
London NW1 5PX

2 August 1994

Dear Sir Geoffrey
I am Woman's Realm Magazine's Official Complainer and I write on behalf of a
Mrs K Rosenfeld.

I enclose for your urgent laboratory analysis a "Touch N'Listen Bambi Book"
which Mrs Rosenfeld purchased from one of your stores. It is the second such
book which Mrs Rosenfeld has bought. The first one not only didn't work but
produced a curious howling sound! Mrs Rosenfeld took it back. The second one
produced a similar racket until Mr Rosenfeld decided to kick it to death. It
now gives off nothing more than an intermittent whimper.

I have a theory about the howling noise. It has derived from one of two sources.
It is either:

   1) the whining of Bambi's ghost distraught at his demise after receiving
      a fatal blow from Mr Rosenfeld's boot or
   2) the by-product of a shoddy toy which gives a whole new meaning to the
      word useless.

Mrs Rosenfeld has wasted a considerable amount of time and energy as a consequence
of this nonsense. Please rectify the situation with an appropriate gesture of
goodwill.

I await your earliest reply.

Yours sincerely

Jasper Griegson

WOOLWORTHS

Woolworths plc
Woolworth House
242/246 Marylebone Road, London NW1 6JL

telephone 071-262 1222
facsimile 071-706 5416
telex 24898

your ref

our ref   direct dialling telephone 071-706

3 August 1994

Dear Mrs Rosenfeld

I have received information from Jasper Griegson at Woman's Realm Magazine via
Kingfisher's Chairman, and have been asked to respond on his behalf.

I was sorry to learn that you have encountered problems with two Touch 'N Listen Bambi
books, and can appreciate your dismay and the inconvenience this will have caused. We have
a strong committment to offering value-for-money products in our stores which work and do
not let people down. The returned book will be passed to our Quality Control Manager in the
toy area and he will investigate and take any action deemed necessary. I have discussed your
findings with him and can confirm that he has had no prior feedback to indicate a quality
problem with this line.

Please accept the enclosed Bambi book which works perfectly. I hope this isn't redundant, but
if you do have one already, you may wish to give this one away as a gift. In addition, to
apologise for your inconvenience, I enclose £5 in gift vouchers for your use the next time you
visit one of our stores.

Thank you for taking steps to bring your concerns to our attention. I hope this unfortunate
experience will not deter you and your family from shopping with us in future.

Yours sincerely

Debra Sharp

Debra Sharp
Customer Relations Manager

cc Chairman, Kingfisher Plc
   J Griegson, Woman's Realm

113

8

If All Else Fails

Imagine the following scenario. You go shopping and spend £100 on a Kenwood Gourmet food processor. You plug it in and it doesn't work. You swear at your spouse, you whack the stupid object with a blunt instrument and then you swear at your spouse again. It still doesn't work. If all else fails you read the instructions. It still doesn't work. You then send the machine to the managing director of Comet who returns it still in a state of disrepair with a dismissive two-line letter written by his personal assistant. What do you do then? Where do you go for justice?

At this point you only have one option and that is to sue the offending company. You don't need a lawyer to do this. The Small Claims Court is supposed to be for everyone's use but the trouble is that most people are afraid to use it. They associate courts with juries, Perry Mason and the death penalty. Your local Small Claims Court is none of these things. Your complaint is generally heard in a pokey DSS-type office with you, your opponent and a balding middle-aged man called a district judge who will bend over backwards to help you. Try it. It's fun. If at the end of the hearing the district judge does put on a black cap and orders you to be taken to a place of execution you know who to complain to. Me.

Talking of death, I have often thought about the logistical difficulties which will inevitably be involved when I push up the daisies. I can't believe for a moment that I'm going to be at all happy with the colour of the coffin lining, let alone the squeaky brake shoes on the back wheels of the hearse. This troubles me. Fortunately, at least one issue has already been resolved. The inscription on my tombstone will read as follows:

RETURN TO SENDER

Although palaeolithic man was born to haul boulders there is no reason why 1994 Beckenham man should do the same.

1 Virginia Street, London E1 9XP. Telephone: 071-782 4000. Telex: 262135.

8th February 1994

Victoria Radice
Managing Director
The Heals Building
196 Tottenham Court Road
London
W1T 9LD

Dear Ms Radice

I am the Sun Newspaper's Official Complainer and I write on behalf of a Mr Clarke.

Very recently Mr Clarke visited your Croydon branch and parted company with 399 smackeroos in order to become the proud owner of a sofa bed. Sofa so good. He lugged the sofabed home much in the same way as prehistoric slaves took boulders to Stonehenge. After expending approximately 4,000 calories of energy in loading, unloading, carrying and hauling the object, Mr Clarke finally sat down and had a cup of tea. When doing so he realised that part of the back of the sofabed had been ripped off. 'Have I been ripped off too?' he thought.

Mr Clarke is a reasonable man and requested an on-site repair or for your company to come and replace the damaged item. Your company declined notifying Mr Clarke that he must repeat the lugging exercise in reverse. Please spare Mr Clarke's spine by organising the hard work to be done that will remedy the problem.

I thank you in advance for your help.

Yours sincerely

Jasper Griegson

habitat
UK

2 March 1994

Dear Mr Griegson

Thank you for your letter outlining the unfortunate plight of Mr Derek Clarke following the purchase of a sofabed from our Croydon store.

I immediately spoke to our store manager, Lloyd Pickering, who straight away contacted Mr Clarke with the result that the faulty sofa was exchanged for a new one.

We certainly do not expect our customers to be personally responsible for transporting faulty sofas back to the stores and I have asked Lloyd Pickering to re-acquaint his staff with Habitat's expectations on this point. If a customer has a problem with a Habitat sofa, then the store will arrange for a member of staff to inspect it at the customer's home and if an exchange or refund is due, the store will of course arrange all the necessary transport.

Thank you very much for bringing this matter to my attention. I have been assured that Mr Clarke is now happy with his purchase and we hope that he has not been deterred from visiting Habitat again.

Yours sincerely

Vittorio Radice
Managing Director

1 Virginia Street, London E1 9XP. Telephone: 071-782 4000. Telex: 262135.

25th November 1993

P C Cohen Esq
Chairman
Courts (Furnishers) plc
The Grange
1 Central Road
Morden, Surrey
SM4 5RX

Dear Mr Cohen

I am the Sun Newspaper's Official Complainer and I write on
behalf of a Mrs W Bagley.

As I recall your advertisement states 'See you all in Courts'.
Mrs Bagley would like to see you in the type of Court at which
justice is dispensed but unfortunately cannot afford the legal
expense. Her problem in essence is that she paid a considerable
sum for a three piece suite in return for which she seems to have
been given three unpredictable porcupines.

I should explain.

Despite the fact the the furniture was bought only two years ago
it appears to sprout springs at the rate of knots. After one
popped out from the side of the settee more dropped out from the
bottom. One of the chairs is projecting its innards in the same
way.

I would be grateful if you would now emulate Mrs Bagley's shoddy
furniture and SPRING into action.

I await your earliest reply.

Yours sincerely

Jasper Griegson

High Street Stores
Mammoth Superstores

The Grange, 1 Central Road, Morden, Surrey SM4 5RX. Telephone: 081-640 3322 Fax: 081-528 7505

Our Ref: SG/EJJ/LLANDUDNO   30 November, 1993

Dear Mr & Mrs Bagley

WITHOUT PREJUDICE

We have recently received a letter from Jasper Griegson of the Sun with regard to your Capricorn suite.   We are sorry that you have had problems with this suite.   Unfortunately due to its age and the lack of care and attention given we are unable to service it further.

However as a gesture of goodwill we have written off the balance outstanding of £301.74 on your Home Plan account with us.   Therefore we have instructed our debt collection agency, Chase 3C, to suspend proceedings and close their files. No records will be retained as to the debt.

Yours sincerely

SARAH GHINN
Assistant Company Secretary

1 Virginia Street, London E1 9XP. Telephone: 071-782 4000. Telex: 262135.

16th December 1993

A K P Smith, Esq
Chairman and Chief Executive
Kingfisher plc
North West House
119 Marylebone Road
London
NW1 5PX

Dear Mr Smith

I am the Sun Newspaper's Official Complainer and I write on
behalf of a Mr D Hoare.

On 2nd November 1991 Mr Hoare purchased a duff JVC video recorder
from a Comet Store at Llansamlet in Swansea. After two years of
battle (see Comet's ref LV/345-34165) Mr Hoare is finally in
possession of a working machine. In the meantime he has had to
suffer (1) weeks on end without a working machine (2) the
destruction of several chewed tapes (3) intolerable inconvenience
and (4) the cost of sending a solicitor's letter to Comet (£58)
which letter finally sparked them into repair mode.

Mr Hoare is not a happy man. Please let me know which of the
following two steps you would now propose taking:-

                    (a) Nothing or
                    (b) Something

I await your earliest reply.

Yours sincerely

Jasper Griegson

KING*F*SHER

22nd December 1993

Alan K P Smith
Chief Executive

Mr Jasper Griegson
The Sun
1 Virginia Street
London
E1 9XP

Dear Mr Griegson

Thank you for writing to me about Mr Hoare, the answer to your question is (b).
Comet will make a direct reponse to Mr Hoare.

Yours sincerely

[signature]

Alan K. P. Smith

Within the human experience some things are immutable: the position of the planets, the ebb and flow of the tides and the fact that eating two king-size Mars Bars will make you sick. Other things, however, can be changed – including the attitude of stubborn companies who have no regard for the suffering of their customers.

1 Virginia Street, London E1 9XP. Telephone: 071-782 4000. Telex: 262135.

2nd February 1994

Alberto Bertali Esq
Managing Director
Kelco Candy Limited
Merseyside

Dear Bertali

I am the Sun Newspaper's Official Complainer and I write on
behalf of one of our readers Mrs Cochrane who lives in Scotland.

Mrs Cochrane's complaint is that your company is blowing hot and
cold. Let me explain. She purchased one of your frost-free
freezers in April last year. In early December it failed and as
a consequence defrosted hundreds of pounds worth of Mrs
Cochrane's Christmas shopping. When Mrs Cochrane asked for an
explanation she was told that her machine would not operate in a
room where the temperature drops below 7 degrees celsius! Are
you serious? Does she really have to keep her house hot in order
to keep her freezer cold?

As you may be aware Scotland is not East Africa. Due to factors
beyond Mrs Cochrane's control the planet Earth is positioned in
such a way (vis a vis the Sun) that the temperature in Scotland
can fall below a balmy 7 degrees in Winter.

What would you suggest Mrs Cochrane should do? Whilst you make
up your mind she is running up a ridiculous nocturnal heating
bill.

I await your earliest reply.

Yours sincerely

Jasper Griegson

Kelco Ltd

Registered Office • New Chester Road
Bromborough • Wirral
Merseyside • L62 3PE

Tel: 051-334 2781
Fax: 051-334 0185
051-334 9056
V.A.T. Reg. No. 482 2497 27

8 FEBRUARY 1994

Manufacturers of

Candy
Kelvinator
ZEROWATT

Domestic Appliances

Dear Mr Griegson

RE   YOUR CORRESPONDENCE REFERENCE NO C114

In response to your letter of February 2 1994 regarding Mrs Cochrane's Candy fridge/freezer please find attached a detailed explanation of the conditions which cause fridge/freezers to automatically defrost in addition to the solution to the very unusual problem.

You are free to print this information. However, I would like to stress that this is not a design fault and nor is it a 'syndrome' peculiar to Candy – most manufacturers offer the same inherent design and advice.

As a conscientious Company we have developed the additional kit mentioned to assist our customers who are forced to locate their fridge/freezer in an area where ambient temperatures are below those dictated by the British Standards. The kit will lower the minimum operating temperature of the fridge/freezer by several degrees and is normally offered as an optional extra – chargeable to the customer.

In this instance as a gesture of goodwill on behalf of Candy Domestic Appliances, we are prepared to supply and fit the kit on a F.O.C. basis.

On a more personal level I would like to say that I found the sarcastic nature of your letter both insulting and unnecessary. Candy is a reputable company and we would have responded to your enquiry in exactly the same manner had a polite letter been received from yourself which pointed out the facts.

I hope that this explanation satisfies your query. Please don't hesitate to call if you need any further information.

Yours sincerely

C Darwen
Marketing Director

If you are the owner of a Rover motor car you may or may not have been happy when it was announced that Rover had been taken over by BMW. Not surprisingly, I had some sympathy with those Rover owners who were not happy. In expressing my dissatisfaction I employed the greatest degree of tact and even managed to avoid mentioning the war. Nearly.

1 Virginia Street, London E1 9XP. Telephone: 071-782 4000. Telex: 262135.

Neil Johnson Esq.
European Operations Director
Rover Group Holdings
Birmingham
B37 7HQ

2nd February 1994

Dear Mr Johnson

I am the Sun Newspaper's Official Complainer and I write on behalf of a number of our readers who have contacted me to complain about the recent takeover of Rover. This is a subject close to my own heart since it I too have a car manufactured by your company parked in my driveway.

The problem in essence is this. On Sunday night I (like thousands of others) was the proud driver of a Rover. By Monday lunchtime I had become a BMW owner with all that that entails.

If I had ever fostered a longing for cold teutonic steel and firm (almost back-breaking) seats I would have invested in a German machine many years ago. Instead I put my money on a good old British work-horse of a car which carries none of the polished but severe undertones portrayed by its Prussian competitors.

In short, I feel cheated. It's a bit like buying a pound of pork sausages and being given a kilo of bratwurst. Although I've got nothing against the Germans I'd rather not be piloting the automobile equivalent of a Messerschmitt.

In all the circumstances I would be most grateful indeed if you would apologise to all the people who have now become unwilling members of a club to which they would rather not belong.

I thank you in advance for your interest.

Yours sincerely

J. Griegson

Jasper Griegson

Sadly, Mr Johnson did not reply to this letter. Rover did send out a circular letter to all Rover owners but it discreetly avoided the true causes of Anglo-German antagonism: Geoff Hurst's disputed goal (1966); Gerd Müller's indisputable goal (1970) and the grandiose career objectives of a short man with a Charlie Chaplin moustache.

1 Virginia Street, London E1 9XP. Telephone: 071-782 4000. Telex: 262135.

5th November 1993

Sir Ian Maclaurin
Chairman
Tesco plc
Cheshunt
Herts EN8 9SL

Dear Sir Ian

Re   Dead Beetle

I am the Sun Newspaper's Official Complainer and I wish to register a complaint on behalf of a Mrs V Marsh.

The problem in essence is this. Mrs Marsh has in her freezer a dead beetle (hereinafter referred to as 'Bob'). Allow me to eliminate a few possibilities.

Bob is not part of an experiment in insect cryonics.

Bob is not going to be used to garnish the Marsh household's frozen pizza.

Bob is not a welcome addition to the Marsh household.

Bob arrived courtesy of a tin of Smedley's garden peas purchased at Mrs Marsh's local Tesco store. She still has the tin.

I would suggest a dignified burial for Bob and a gesture of goodwill to Mrs Marsh. Any thoughts?

Yours sincerely

Jasper Griegson

TESCO

Tesco House
P.O. Box 18,
Delamare Road,
Cheshunt,
Waltham Cross,
Herts, EN8 9SL

Switchboard: 0992 - 632222
Facsimile: 0992 - 644961
Telex: 24138 Tesco G

Ext:

2 December 1993

Dear Mr Griegson

I am writing further to your recent letter regarding the problem that Mrs Marsh experienced after purchasing a tin of Smedley Garden Peas.

Firstly I would like to confirm that the suppliers, Haywards Foods Ltd, have picked up the produce and 'Bob' from Mrs Marsh so that they may undertake a full investigation. They have subsequently written direct to Mrs Marsh with an explanation and sent a gesture of goodwill payment of £25.

Assuring you of our best attention at all times.

Yours sincerely
For and on behalf of
Tesco Stores Limited

N E Bowman
Customer Relations Director

A Final Thought

I am confident that by the time I finally arrive at the Pearly Gates (I wonder if the hinges will need oiling?) I will have been replaced on earth. Only the other day my eldest daughter made a demand with menaces for sweets, which suggests that she is carrying my curiously defective genes. Instead of sulking, as most children would do when refused confectionery, she handed me the following note:

> 'Unless I receive a packet of Jelly Tots within two working days I will have no option . . .'

A new and more virulent strain of Jasper would appear to have already been created.